NOTTINGHAM FRENCH STUDIES

VOLUME 54   NUMBER 3   AUTUMN 2015

Still French? France and the Challenge of Diversity, 1985–2015

Edited by Alec G. Hargreaves

This publication is available as a book (ISBN: 9781474406604) or as a single issue or part of a subscription to *Nottingham French Studies*, Volume 54 (ISSN: 0029-4586). Please visit www.euppublishing.com/journal/nfs for more information.

Subscription rates for 2016

Three issues per year, published in March, July, and December

		Tier	UK	EUR	RoW	N. America
Institutions	Print& online	1	£106.00	£116.95	£123.85	$204.50
		2	£132.50	£143.45	£150.35	$248.00
		3	£165.50	£176.45	£183.35	$302.50
		4	£199.00	£209.95	£216.85	$358.00
		5	£225.00	£235.95	£242.85	$400.50
	Online	1	£90.00	£90.00	£90.00	$148.50
		2	£112.50	£112.50	£112.50	$185.50
		3	£141.00	£141.00	£141.00	$232.50
		4	£169.00	£169.00	£169.00	$279.00
		5	£190.50	£190.50	£190.50	$314.50
	Premium print & online	1	£132.50	£143.45	£148.55	$245.00
		2	£166.00	£176.95	£182.05	$300.50
		3	£207.00	£217.95	£223.05	$368.00
		4	£249.50	£260.45	£265.55	$438.00
		5	£281.50	£292.45	£297.55	$491.00
	Premium online	1	£116.50	£116.50	£116.50	$192.00
		2	£146.50	£146.50	£146.50	$241.50
		3	£183.00	£183.00	£183.00	$302.00
		4	£219.00	£219.00	£219.00	$361.50
		5	£247.00	£247.00	£247.00	$407.50
	Additional print volumes		£103.50	£104.00	£110.00	$181.50
	Single issues		£49.00	£52.50	£55.00	$91.00
Individuals	Print		£48.00	£59.00	£66.00	$112.00
	Online		£48.00	£48.00	£48.00	$81.50
	Print & online		£59.00	£70.00	£77.00	$131.00
	Premium online		£62.50	£62.50	£62.50	$106.50
	Premium print & online		£73.50	£84.50	£91.50	$155.50
	Back issues/single copies		£17.50	£21.00	£23.50	$40.00

How to order

Subscriptions can be accepted for complete volumes only. Print prices include packing and airmail for subscribers outside the UK. Volumes back to the year 2000 are included in online prices. Print back volumes/single issues will be charged at the print rates stated above (vol. 51 onwards). Enquiries concerning back volumes/issues up to vol. 50 inclusive should be addressed to Beth Yearsley, Secretary to the Board of *Nottingham French Studies*, Department of French and Francophone Studies, School of Cultures, Languages and Area Studies, University of Nottingham, Nottingham NG7 2RD; email: nfs@nottingham.ac.uk

All orders must be accompanied by the correct payment. You can pay by cheque in Pounds Sterling or US Dollars, bank transfer, Direct Debit or Credit/Debit Card. The individual rate applies only when a subscription is paid for with a personal cheque or credit card. Please make your cheques payable to Edinburgh University Press Ltd. Sterling cheques must be drawn on a UK bank account.

Orders for subscriptions and back issues can be placed by telephone, on +44(0)131 650 4196, by fax on +44(0)131 662 3286, using your Visa or Mastercard credit cards, or by email on journals@eup.ed.ac.uk. Don't forget to include the expiry date of your card, and the address that the card is registered to. Alternatively, you can use the online order form at www.euppublishing.com/page/nfs/subscribe.

Requests for sample copies, subscription enquiries, and changes of address should be sent to Journals Department, Edinburgh University Press, The Tun – Holyrood Road, Edinburgh EH8 8PJ; email: journals@eup.ed.ac.uk

NOTTINGHAM FRENCH STUDIES

VOLUME 54   NUMBER 3   AUTUMN 2015

CONTENTS

Special Issues of *Nottingham French Studies*

Pierre Reverdy: 1889–1989
edited by Bernard McGuirk
28:2 (Autumn 1989)

The Abbé Prévost 1697–1763
edited by R A Francis
29:2 (Autumn 1990)

Arthurian Romance
edited by Roger Middleton
30:2 (Autumn 1991)

Culture and Class in France in the 1930s
edited by Rosemary Chapman
31:2 (Autumn 1992)

French Cinema
edited by Russell King
32:1 (Spring 1993)

Molière
edited by Stephen Bamforth
33:1 (Spring 1994)

Hervé Guibert
edited by Jean-Pierre Boulé
34:1 (Spring 1995)

Ionesco
edited by Steve Smith
35:1 (Spring 1996)

Roland Barthes
edited by Diana Knight
36:1 (Spring 1997)

French Erotic Fiction: Ideologies of Desire
edited by Jean Mainil
37:1 (Spring 1998)

Fortune and Women in Medieval Literature
edited by Katie Attwood
38:2 (Autumn 1999)

Errances Urbaines
edited by Jean-Xavier Ridon
39:1 (Spring 2000)

Gender and Francophone Writing
edited by Nicki Hitchcott
40:1 (Spring 2001)

French Fiction in the 1990s
edited by Margaret-Anne Hutton
41:1 (Spring 2002)

*Thinking in Dialogue: The role
of the interview in post-war French thought*
edited by Christopher Johnson
42:1 (Spring 2003)

Jazz Adventures in French Culture
edited by Jacqueline Dutton and Colin
Nettelbeck
43:1 (Spring 2004)

*Irreconcilable differences? Centre, Periphery
and the Space Between in French history*
edited by Paul Smith
44:1 (Spring 2005)

France, America and the Modern
edited by Jackie Clarke and Carole Sweeney
44:3 (Autumn 2005)

*Focalizing the Body:
Recent Women's Writing and
Filmmaking in France*
edited by Gill Rye and Carrie Tarr
45:3 (Autumn 2006)

*Sociolinguistic Variation and
Change in France*
edited by David Hornsby and Mikaël Jamin
46:2 (Summer 2007)

Terror and Psychoanalysis
edited by Lynsey Russell-Watts with Lisa
Walsh
46:3 (Autumn 2007)

*'Mythologies' at 50: Barthes and Popular
Culture*
edited by Douglas Smith
47:2 (Summer 2008)

*Identification before Freud: French
Perspectives*
edited by Joseph Harris
47:3 (Autumn 2008)

*Annie Ernaux: Socio-Ethnographer of
Contemporary France*
edited by Alison S. Fell and Edward Welch
48:2 (Spring 2009)

*Enlightenment and Narrative: Essays in
Honour of Richard A. Francis by Colleagues
and Friends*
edited by Philip Robinson
48:3 (Autumn 2009)

Future Issues

Nottingham French Studies 54.3 (2015): 227–237
DOI: 10.3366/nfs.2015.0123
© University of Nottingham
www.euppublishing.com/journal/nfs

INTRODUCTION: STILL FRENCH?

ALEC G. HARGREAVES

In a provocative 1985 cover story featuring the face of Marianne obscured by an Islamic veil, *Le Figaro magazine* asked: 'Serons-nous encore français dans 30 ans?'[1] With those thirty years now spanned, where does France stand in relation to the fears, challenges and opportunities associated with changing perceptions of ethnic and cultural diversity? Is the France of 2015 still French in the same way or to the same degree as the France of 1985? Where do the most significant challenges to 'Frenchness' now lie? In Islamism? In the disadvantaged multi-ethnic *banlieues*? In European integration? In American hegemony? Is 'Frenchness' itself, championed by political elites under the banner of 'l'exception culturelle', an outmoded concept, destined to wither in the face of transnational forces? These are among the key issues addressed in this special issue of *Nottingham French Studies*, based on papers presented at a conference hosted by the Department of French and Francophone Studies at the University of Nottingham in March 2015.

Contextualizing the Other

Had *Le Figaro magazine* asked its cover story question twenty or thirty years earlier, it would certainly not have been framed around a perceived Islamic threat. In the decades that followed the Second World War, Islam attracted little attention except as an undercurrent in the nationalist movements that drove the tide of decolonization. With the end of empire sealed following Algerian independence in 1962, uncertainty over France's future was framed primarily by the Cold War rivalry that dominated post-war international politics and that helped to shape party political cleavages within France. In the eyes of many the ideology of the Soviet Union, relayed within the hexagon by the French Communist Party, constituted a fearsome threat not only to the capitalist economic system but also to French values of liberal humanism. In the view of others, including not only the PCF but also President de Gaulle, there was more to fear from the military, economic and cultural hegemony of the United States. Fears of Americanization gained widespread currency in Étiemble's *Parlez-vous franglais?* (1964),

---

1.   'Dossier immigration: Serons-nous encore français dans 30 ans?', *Le Figaro magazine*, 26 October 1985. The dossier featured on the cover was published on pp. 123–132; cited hereafter as *FM*.

Jean-Jacques Servan-Schreiber's *Le Défi américain* (1967) and the PCF's denunciations of 'coca-colonisation'.

Even before the collapse of the Soviet bloc in 1989 ended the Cold War, French political elites began to perceive significant challenges emanating from other quarters. The oil crises of 1973 and 1979 revealed the vulnerability of Western economies, including that of France, to politically-motivated pressures from oil-rich Middle Eastern states. Soaring oil prices put an end to France's *trente glorieuses*, triggering rising unemployment and with it widespread economic insecurity. After the 1973 crisis, grounded in spillover from the Israeli-Palestinian conflict, the crisis of 1979 added a new element: the Islamist political agenda championed by the Iranian revolution of that year.

Both crises impacted significantly on perceptions of immigrant minorities within France. Concerns over unemployment led in 1974 to an official ban on labour migration by non-Europeans, large numbers of whom had come from former French colonies in North and sub-Saharan Africa to fill labour shortages during the post-war economic boom. With this policy switch, these groups now came to be widely perceived as causes of unemployment and as a costly drain on social support systems. These economic anxieties were compounded by new concerns following the Iranian revolution, which drew attention for the first time to the fact that most postcolonial migrants in France were Muslims. While most of France's Muslims were Sunnis from North and West Africa, with no direct connection with the Shia branch of Islam in the name of which the Ayatollah Khomeini had led the Iranian revolution in 1979, this distinction was frequently elided in political and media discourse. In the course of the 1980s, France's Muslim population – the largest in western Europe – became the focal point in an upsurge of identity politics exemplified in the rise of the extreme-right Front National (FN), which has remained a core component of the political landscape for the past thirty years.

If this shift was crystallized in the veiled Marianne featured in 1985 on the cover of the right-of-centre *Figaro magazine*, politicians on the both the left and right had been paving the way for this over a number of years. Early in 1983, Socialist Prime Minister Pierre Mauroy blamed strikes in the automobile industry on immigrant workers 'agités par des groupes religieux et politiques qui se déterminent en fonction de critères ayant peu à voir avec la réalité sociale française'.[2] Mauroy adduced no evidence in support of this claim. Nor did Interior Minister Gaston Defferre when he denounced more specifically the alleged role

---

2.   Remarks by Pierre Mauroy interviewed in *Nord-Éclair*, 28 January 1983, quoted in Catherine Wihtol de Wenden, *Les Immigrés et la politique: cent-cinquante ans d'évolution* (Paris: Presses de la FNSP, 1988), p. 360.

played in the strikes by 'intégristes [...] chiites',[3] implying that the French economy was being sabotaged by Iranian-style Islamists. Following the electoral breakthrough of the FN, initially in local elections in 1983 and then in the European elections of 1984, centre-right politicians began to copy Jean-Marie Le Pen's policies in the hope of stemming the loss to the extreme-right of voters on whom they had previously been able to count. In this way immigrants and their descendants, blamed by the FN as the source of all of France's ills, became increasingly stigmatized not only on economic grounds but also because of the alleged need to protect 'French identity' from alien cultural influences. Thus in the spring of 1985, the centre-right UDF and RPR parties included in their joint electoral platform a pledge to reform French nationality laws in such a way as to exclude the children of immigrants from automatic access to French citizenship on the grounds that supposed cultural differences – essentially those associated with Islam – cast doubts on their loyalty to France.

The thirty years that have elapsed since then have been punctuated by a still ongoing series of policy debates and initiatives fired by concerns over the supposed threat posed by Islam. These include the centre-right's initially unsuccessful attempt to change nationality laws in 1986, the elaborate public hearings conducted by a specially appointed Commission de la nationalité the following year, the huge controversy ignited in 1989 over the wearing of Islamic headscarves in state schools, the nationality law reform pushed through by the centre-right in 1993, its reversal when the left returned to power in 1997, the anti-headscarf law of 2004, the government-orchestrated debate on national identity in 2009–10, the anti-burqa law adopted in 2010, and current stirrings by politicians on both the right and left who want the ban on headscarves to be extended from schools into universities. The heated nature of these discussions is vividly illustrated in Yvan Gastaut's analysis of the elaborately structured but often unruly debate on French national identity launched in 2009.

Islam is not the only Other feared in France today. In the face of migratory inflows that are, as Catherine Wihtol de Wenden shows, at the same time more European than is often thought and increasingly global in scope, public antipathy has been stirred against a range of targets. While anti-Americanism has diminished significantly in the past three decades, recent years have brought an in many ways unexpected rise in hostility towards the European Union. Witness the 'no' vote in the 2005 referendum on the proposed European constitution, the refocusing of the FN's programme on withdrawal from the EU since Marine Le Pen succeeded her father at the head of the party in 2011, and recent moral panics over Roma entering France from Eastern Europe. But if the EU is increasingly blamed for the economic ills affecting France, postcolonial minorities, especially

---

3.   Michel Noblecourt, 'Une phrase de trop', *Le Monde*, 30–31 January 1983; 'Immigrés et islamisme, quelle mouche a piqué Mauroy et Defferre?', *Libération*, 1 February 1983.

those of Muslim heritage, are perceived ever more strongly as the main threat to the integrity of French national identity, a perception that has been reinforced by the jihadist murders carried out in January 2015 targeting *Charlie Hebdo* journalists, police officers and Jews. Until recently, 'Arabs' and 'Muslims' were widely seen as synonymous in popular discourse, reflecting the demographic dominance of North Africans among the Muslim population in France, and those groups were consistently viewed more negatively than 'Blacks', who in popular thinking were not generally associated with Islam.[4] While 'Blacks' from French territories in the Caribbean are generally Christian and/or secular in outlook, a significant proportion of those from sub-Saharan Africa are Muslims. Growing awareness of this has tended to lower the standing of 'Blacks' in public esteem and as David Murphy notes, the role played by Amedy Coulibaly, the son of Malian immigrants, in the January 2015 killings has accentuated this trend.

Paradoxes of 'diversity'
While decentralization has since the 1980s reinvigorated regional minorities who until then had been confined to the margins of French history, the traditionally centralized nature of the French state has remained inhospitable towards foreign cultural influences, including those associated with minorities of immigrant origin. During the early decades of the Fifth Republic, there was a broad political consensus around the idea of protecting what came to be known as the 'French exception', understood as denoting both the sovereignty of the nation-state and the uniqueness of French culture.[5] While de Gaulle sought to protect national sovereignty by remaining aloof from NATO and slowing the pace of European integration, his centrist and Socialist successors took off the brakes, ceding portions of French sovereignty in economic and related matters to the European Union in the hope of better resisting American global dominance. This meant that the Hexagon could be protected from foreign (especially American) cultural imports only by persuading the EU to insist on their exclusion from free trade treaties. In this way, what had previously been referred to as the French exception became transmuted during the 1990s into 'l'exception culturelle', denoting a means of protecting national cultural markets through agreements reached at European and global levels. Pressing this momentum further, France sought to normalize cultural protectionism by dropping the language of exceptionalism in favour of a Universal Declaration on Cultural Diversity, which was adopted under the auspices of UNESCO in 2001.

---

4.   See the opinion survey data for 1990–2013 in Commission nationale consultative des droits de l'homme, *La Lutte contre le racisme, l'antisémitisme et la xénophobie*, année 2013 (Paris: La Documentation française, 2014), p. 165.

5.   *The French Exception,* ed. by Emmanuel Godin and Tony Chafer (Oxford: Berghahn, 2005).

Simultaneously 'la diversité' was entering the political lexicon in France with reference to developments of a very different nature. During the late 1990s, policy-makers had become increasingly concerned that public order was being threatened by violence arising from disaffection among minority ethnic groups over racial and ethnic discrimination. Beginning in 2000, commitments to ensure fairer treatment of those minorities were presented in the name of 'diversité', which had a gentler and more feel-good resonance than 'anti-discrimination'. In practice the incantation of 'la diversité' was to prove little more than a fig-leaf papering over the lack of effective action against discrimination, fuelling deepening resentment that exploded in the riots of 2005 and the jihadist networks that came to the fore in 2015.[6] Neither should it be thought that the consensus across most of the political spectrum around the slogan of 'diversité' betokened a commitment to multiculturalism, a notion that was and still is virtually taboo in French political discourse.[7]

The seeming contradiction between the championing of cultural diversity in the international arena and the rejection of multiculturalism within France is more apparent than real. At both levels, the objective of public policy has been to protect the cultural norms dominant in France, on the one hand against international (especially American) influences and on the other hand against threats (especially Islamic) associated with postcolonial minorities who have settled in France.

Flawed predictions

The alarmist dossier published by *Le Figaro magazine* in 1985 was the work of Gérard-François Dumont, who compiled the data, and Jean Raspail, who wrote the text. Dumont was a young disciple of the demographer Alfred Sauvy, who had been warning for decades that France, as part of the rich North, was in danger of being submerged under population movements emanating from the poor South. Raspail was best known for his novel *Le Camp des saints*, in which he had imagined France being overrun by an uncontrolled influx of immigrants from what Sauvy had called the Third World.[8]

In the projections produced by Dumont and Raspail, the population of France is divided into two categories: on the one hand French nationals of French and European origin and on the other hand, foreigners of non-European origin, for whom the acronym E.N.E. (Étrangers non européens) is invented. Dumont

---

6. Alec G. Hargreaves, 'French Muslims and the Middle East', *Contemporary French Civilization*, 40:2 (Summer 2015), 235–54.

7. Michel Wieviorka, *La Diversité: rapport à la Ministre de l'Enseignement supérieur et de la recherche* (Paris: Robert Laffont, 2008).

8. Jean Raspail, *Le Camp des saints* (Paris: Robert Laffont, 1973).

assumes that the fertility of non-Europeans in France will be three times the rate of the rest of the population, and that each year there will be a net increase of between 59,000 and 100,000 immigrants from non-European countries. He includes in the E.N.E. category of 'foreigners' the children of non-European immigrants, most of whom are in fact French nationals by virtue of being born in France. On this basis Dumont predicts that by 2015 there will be between 9.5 and 12.8 million E.N.E., 'de culture et de religion islamique à 90%', accounting for between 17 and 22 per cent of a total population approaching 60 million. Among the consequences predicted by Raspail are that by 2015 Islam will be 'la première religion de France', while in the political arena Muslims will constitute 'le premier parti de France', Islamic law will prevail in large swathes of the country, spelling the end of 'le vieux pays chrétien', millions of Muslims will demonstrate in the streets demanding state-subsidized Islamic schools, and a system of de facto apartheid will divide Muslims from non-Muslims with conflicts between these two supposed communities becoming endemic in daily life (*FM*, pp. 126–9).

If these predictions have proven largely erroneous, this is because they were based on numerous faulty assumptions. In census data published by INSEE in 2012, non-European immigrants (most of whom remained foreigners) and their children (most of whom were French nationals) accounted for 6.7 million or 11 per cent of metropolitan France's total population of 62.5 million.[9] This was at most only half the level predicted by Dumont. These quantitative errors were compounded by major qualitative flaws in the lurid vision of the future expounded by Raspail grounded in simplistic notions of cultural essentialism that border on biological racism. His predictions assumed that the children and grand-children of Muslim migrants would mechanically replicate the cultural norms of their parents and grand-parents, resisting any form of mixing, integration or assimilation in their dealings with the majority ethnic population, preferring to lead their lives as a separate Muslim community hostile to the cultural norms hitherto dominant in France.

It would be difficult for Raspail to have got things more comprehensively wrong. While Islam is now the second largest religion in France, its adherents remain far smaller in number than those of Catholicism. Numerous studies have shown that the children of Muslim immigrants, like those from non-Muslim immigrant backgrounds, are far closer to the cultural norms of their majority ethnic peers than to those of their migrant parents, and their material aspirations – in large measure, those of the consumer society – are very similar

---

9.   INSEE, *Immigrés et descendants d'immigrés en France*, édition 2012. < http://www.in-see.fr/fr/publications-et-services/sommaire.asp?reg_id=0&ref_id=IMMFRA12> [accessed 29 May 2015].

to those of the majority ethnic population.[10] But they have been prevented from participating on an equal footing in French society by widespread discrimination in employment, housing and many other fields. Exasperated by the failure of the Republic to live up to its commitment to ensure equality before the law for all persons irrespective of their origins, postcolonial minorities have come increasingly to despair of the political process, resulting in low levels of electoral registration and turnout. In the France of 2015, there is no organized Muslim party of any political significance, whereas the party now credited with the largest share of the national vote is the FN, whose platform is based on anti-immigrant rhetoric. Far from Koranic law replacing that of the Republic, Parliament has in recent years passed a series of laws modifying the code of *laïcité* so as to restrict the right of Muslims to display their religious convictions publicly. While thousands of Catholic schools and dozens of Jewish schools enjoy state funding, only two Islamic schools have been granted that status. Demonstrations by Muslims have seldom mobilized more than a few hundred or at most a few thousand participants, in sharp contrast with the millions of mainly 'white', non-Muslim demonstrators who joined the 'Je suis Charlie' rally held in Paris on 11 January 2015. In the wake of that rally, Prime Minister Manuel Valls lamented that 'un apartheid territorial, social, ethnique, [...] s'est imposé à notre pays'.[11] While this may appear at first sight to vindicate Raspail's warning of 'une sorte d'apartheid de fait subi puis voulu par les deux communautés' (*FM*, p. 129), it is important to note that this has resulted far less from self-segregation or domination imposed by Muslims, as predicted by Raspail, than from social exclusion suffered by minority ethnic groups at the hands of members of the majority ethnic population.

The corrosive effects of discrimination in excluding minority groups from participation in the life of the nation, which are highlighted by Azouz Begag, drawing on his personal, professional and governmental experiences, are such that it is hardly surprising if there was reticence in certain quarters concerning calls for displays of national unity in the wake of the *Charlie Hebdo* and Hyper Cacher killings. In scores of schools in the *banlieues*, pupils refused to observe a minute's silence in respect for the victims,[12] thousands of 'JeNeSuisPasCharlie' tweets

---

10. Bruno Etienne, *La France et l'islam* (Paris: Hachette, 1989); Michèle Tribalat, *Faire France: une enquête sur les immigrés et leurs enfants* (Paris: La Découverte, 1995); Sylvain Brouard and Vincent Tiberj, *Français comme les autres? Enquête sur les citoyens d'origine maghrébine, africaine et turque* (Paris: FNSP, 2005).

11. 'Manuel Valls évoque "un apartheid territorial, social, ethnique" en France', *Le Monde*, 20 January 2015.

12. Mattea Battaglia and Benoit Floc'h, 'À Saint-Denis, collégiens et lycéens ne sont pas tous "Charlie"', *Le Monde*, 10 January 2015.

were sent in the days immediately following the attacks,[13] and few minority ethnic faces were visible in the huge rally of January 11.[14] The day afterwards, a collective of associations based in the *banlieues* organized its own rally against violence and stigmatization outside the Préfecture of Seine-Saint-Denis, the poorest *département* in France and epicentre of the 2005 riots. Spokesperson Mohamed Mechmouche said the site of the rally – 'un lieu de la République' – had been deliberately chosen: 'Cette République, on ne s'en éloigne pas, on veut seulement s'en rapprocher. [...] Avec les événements du 7 janvier [i.e. the *Charlie Hebdo* murders], on est confrontés à quelque chose qui avait été dit depuis longtemps par les acteurs de terrain. Il faut qu'on se parle sur ce qu'on vit depuis 30 ans.'[15] Mechmouche added: 'Ces prochains jours, une frange de la population va vite retourner à son individualisme. Une autre, dans les quartiers populaires, va vite être rattrapée par la réalité: le chômage, les discriminations, les gamins qui décrochent du système scolaire, le "deal" dans les quartiers qu'on subit...'[16]

Forces of exclusion

The marginalization of minorities in the *banlieues* has been driven by prejudiced attitudes and discriminatory practices not only in civil society but also within the state itself, including law enforcement agencies. Research funded by the Open Society Justice Initiative has demonstrated the magnitude of racial profiling in police identity checks, a long-standing grievance among minority ethnic youths. Observations conducted in 2007–8 found that, compared with whites, Blacks were four times more likely and Arabs seven times more likely to be subjected to identity checks.[17] No effective action has been taken by governments of either left or right against these discriminatory practices.

While serving as Interior Minister, France's highest law enforcement officer, Brice Hortefeux was himself convicted in 2010 of racial insults against Arabs, yet he remained in post. It is true that Hortefeux's conviction was overturned the following year on a legal technicality. But the appeal court confirmed the racist

---

13. Camile Kaelblen, 'Etre ou ne pas être Charlie: les hashtags en chiffres', *Libération*, 13 January 2015.

14. Laurent Chabrun, 'Benjamin Stora: "Il faut enseigner l'histoire du Maghreb et de l'islam en France"', *L'Express*, 16 January 2015.

15. Pierre Benetti, '"Il faut pas laisser les jeunes de banlieue de côté"', *Libération*, 12 January 2015.

16. 'Mohamed Mechmache: "La banlieue n'est pas un réservoir de coupables, elle est une partie de la solution"', *L'Humanité*, 12 January 2015.

17. Open Society Justice Initiative, *Police et minorités visibles: les contrôles d'identité à Paris* (New York, Open Society Institute, 2009): < http://www.opensocietyfoundations. org/sites/default/files/french_20090630_0_0.pdf> [accessed 14 September 2014].

nature of Hortefeux's remarks while ruling that as the comments – made informally to a group of UMP militants and filmed by chance by a TV crew – were not technically made in public they fell outside the legal grounds on which he had been charged.[18] At a higher level still, in 1991 former Prime Minister, then Mayor of Paris and future President, Jacques Chirac sympathized with those who disliked what he called 'le bruit et l'odeur' arising from an 'overdose' of African immigrants.[19] A few months later former President Valéry Giscard d'Estaing likened immigration to an invasion,[20] a word that in France resonates with memories of the Nazi occupation. In 2007 Interior Minister Nicolas Sarkozy launched his successful presidential election campaign by vowing on nationwide TV to ensure that that Muslims would not be permitted to slaughter sheep in their bathtubs, crudely recycling an urban myth pandering to Islamophobic prejudices.[21] He also pledged to set up a Ministry for Immigration and National Identity, thereby institutionalizing the supposed need to protect French national identity from the threat of immigration. The man he appointed to head that ministry, turncoat Socialist Eric Besson, duly launched a government-organized debate on French national identity that quickly produced an outpouring of Islamophobic sentiments.

Intellectuals, and a fortiori those who style themselves as philosophers, might be expected to think and speak with greater insight and finesse. To the contrary, some of the most prominent of those intellectuals have seized countless media opportunities to recycle the crude phobias voiced in 1985 by *Le Figaro magazine* against minorities who, they now claim, threaten to destroy French identity in the next thirty years if not sooner. Recent examples include Renaud Camus's theory of 'le grand remplacement', Alain Finkielkraut's essay on *L'Identité malheureuse*, and Éric Zemmour's best-seller *Le Suicide français*, all of which contribute to a climate in which dominant discourses legitimize the exclusionary treatment of postcolonial, especially Muslim, minorities.[22]

---

18. 'Brice Hortefeux définitivement relaxé pour ses propos sur les Arabes', *Le Monde*, 27 Novembre 2012.

19. A filmed record of Chirac's remarks, made on 19 June 1991, may be viewed on Youtube: < https://www.youtube.com/watch?v=e4pun9Cdp6Q> [accessed 30 May 2015].

20. Cover story in *Le Figaro magazine*, 21 September 1991, illustrated once again with an image of a veiled Marianne.

21. TF1, 5 February 2007, 'J'ai une question à vous poser'.

22. Renaud Camus, *Le Grand Remplacement* (Neuilly-sur-Seine: David Reinharc, 2011), Alain Finkielkraut, *L'Identité malheureuse* (Paris: Stock, 2013), Éric Zemmour, *Le Suicide français* (Paris: Albin Michel, 2014). This climate has also been nourished by media coverage of Michel Houellebecq's best-selling novel *Soumission* (Paris: Flammarion, 2015), which imagines the election of a Muslim as French president in 2022, followed by the introduction of sharia law.

Gates of opportunity

Despite these entrenched patterns of prejudice and discrimination, significant numbers of young men and women from minority ethnic backgrounds have been willing to put their lives on the line in defending the Republic and the values for which it stands. These include volunteers in the armed forces, three of whom – all from North African backgrounds – were slain in Montauban in 2012 by Mohamed Merah before he went on to kill three children and one of their teachers at a Jewish school in Toulouse. Two of the three police officers killed in the January 2015 attacks carried out by young men of North and West African origin were a black policewoman from Martinique, Clarissa Jean-Philippe, and a practising Muslim of Algerian immigrant descent, Ahmed Merabet. As Olivier Roy has observed, 'en France, il y a plus de musulmans dans l'armée, la police et la gendarmerie que dans les réseaux Al-Qaida, sans parler de l'administration, des hôpitaux, du barreau ou de l'enseignement'.[23]

But Muslims and others of postcolonial immigrant descent who have entered these professions remain concentrated in the lower échelons. No intellectuals from France's most disadvantaged minorities enjoy the tiniest fraction of the media exposure routinely granted to the polemical tirades of Finkielkraut and Zemmour. Until 2012, there was not a single *député* of North African Muslim heritage among the 577 members of the Assemblée Nationale. French universities, publishers and critics still remain largely wedded to a binary distinction between 'French' and 'Francophone' literatures that has tended to marginalize writers of postcolonial immigrant origin. In response to concerns that that distinction has tended to perpetuate a neocolonial hierarchy between 'true' French literature by writers of French descent born in the Hexagon and a separate 'Francophone' corpus (generally accorded lesser status) by writers born in former French colonies, a manifesto in favour of a 'Littérature-monde en français' was launched in 2007 with the declared objective of embracing on an equal footing all writing in the French language.[24] The manifesto's 44 signatories did not include a single author born in France of postcolonial immigrant parents, though scores of such writers have entered print since the beginning of the 1980s. Often referred to as 'écrivains de banlieue', a group of these minority ethnic authors styling themselves as the Collectif Qui fait la France? launched their own manifesto a few months later.[25] While those who had signed the 'Littérature-monde' manifesto had set their sights on combining their efforts to advance their visibility on the world stage, members of the Qui fait la France? collective had a far more modest but more immediately pressing aim: to gain recognition as

---

23. Olivier Roy, 'La Peur d'une communauté qui n'existe pas', *Le Monde*, 9 January 2015.
24. 'Pour une "littérature-monde" en français', *Le Monde*, 16 March 2007.
25. Collectif Qui Fait la France?, *Chroniques d'une société annoncée* (Paris: Stock, 2007).

integral parts of the cultural fabric of the country in which they had been born and grown up.

Where the gates of opportunity have been opened more widely, this has generally been less as a result of initiatives taken by intellectuals or politicians – who have been long on grandiose republican rhetoric and short on substantive action in favour of equality – than in response to commercial calculations made by private corporations. In many fields of popular culture such as music, cinema and sport, commercial successes have been based on recognition of the demographic importance of minority ethnic groups and the talents that can be tapped among them. In all of those spheres, younger age groups, among whom ethnic minorities have a large presence, constitute key markets. This was an important factor in the rise of French rap during the 1990s, when it became the most popular form of music among young people of majority as well as minority ethnic origin. The simultaneous proliferation of multiplex cinemas in the *banlieues* tapped into large minority ethnic audiences who were all the more attracted to the box-office to the extent that a growing number of films gave starring roles to young actors from the same backgrounds,[26] though as Carrie Tarr shows, a significant gender gap still remains in this respect. If, in 2002, Jamel Debbouze became France's best paid cinema actor, edging Gérard Depardieu into second place, this was due in part to his ability to attract large minority as well as majority ethnic audiences. While the overall pattern is still uneven, the triumph of France's multi-ethnic soccer team in the 1998 World Cup is, as Philip Dine demonstrates, just one among numerous examples of the successes that can be gained in the sporting arena and elsewhere when the nation draws on the talents of all its members, irrespective of their ethnic origins.

Conclusion

The changes that have taken place in every field of French culture in the past thirty years have made it necessary to rethink the terms in which, as scholars, we conceive and theorize French studies. A key feature of this has been the rise of 'Francophone' studies in response to the growth of French-language cultures outside the Hexagon, mainly in former colonies. As Charles Forsdick shows, the porosity of the boundaries between these and other spaces is now such that 'Frenchness' is literally unthinkable as a freestanding entity. Not the least of the paradoxes involved in this is that the threats that many now perceive within the Hexagon are rooted in a dynamic that began when France expanded in earlier times beyond its boundaries. France is certainly still French, though not in exactly the same way as thirty years ago. But neither was it ever 'purely' French, nor can it ever be in the future.

---

26. Julien Gaertner, 'Le Préjugé se vend bien: Arabes et Asiatiques dans le discours ciné-matographique français', *Migrations-société*, 19:109 (January 2007), 163–73.

Nottingham French Studies 54.3 (2015): 238–252
DOI: 10.3366/nfs.2015.0124
© University of Nottingham
www.euppublishing.com/journal/nfs

THE EMERGENCE OF A BLACK FRANCE, 1985–2015: HISTORY, RACE AND IDENTITY

DAVID MURPHY

On the morning of 8 January 2015, less than twenty-four hours after the violent attack on the offices of the satirical magazine *Charlie Hebdo* by the brothers, Said and Chérif Kouachi, an unnamed black gunman shot dead a policewoman in the Parisian suburb of Montrouge. The murderer, later identified as Amedy Coulibaly, would the very next day launch an anti-Semitic attack on the *Hyper Cacher* supermarket at the Porte de Vincennes killing four people. Coulibaly was born in France to parents from Mali, and grew up on the notorious housing estate, La Grande-Borne, in Grigny, south of Paris.[1] Like so many French *cités*, La Grande-Borne was imagined by its planners in the 1960s as a social utopia, the ideal dormitory town; its sinuous, colourful buildings would serve as the antithesis of grey postwar brutalist architecture. Instead, the *cité*, which houses 11,000 people (including a large black population), has become synonymous with poverty, drug dealing, arms trafficking, youth criminality and attacks on police, as well as arson attacks on public buildings. Unemployment amongst the inhabitants of La Grande-Borne is estimated to reach the dizzying heights of over 40%: it has become the classic example of the state housing scheme as social dustbin.

By chance, one of the shop assistants in *Hyper Cacher* on that fateful day was Lassana Bathily, a 24-year-old Muslim immigrant from Mali, who risked his own life to save some of the shop's customers, hiding them in a fridge in the basement. In a rather telling irony, the police initially thought that Bathily was one of Coulibaly's conspirators and, having finally escaped the hostage situation, the unfortunate shop assistant spent his first 90 minutes of freedom hand-cuffed in police custody. However, as the siege ended, relieved customers told police and reporters of Bathily's heroism and he soon found himself lauded by the French public and a political elite desperate to draw some positives from the most harrowing week in recent French history. An online petition launched two days after the supermarket attack by the *Conseil Représentatif des Associations Noires* (CRAN) had, within a week, received over 300,000 signatures supporting its request that the President should grant Bathily French citizenship and award him

---

1. Angélique Chrisafis, 'Charlie Hebdo Attackers: born, raised and radicalized in Paris', *The Guardian*, 12 January 2015: <www.theguardian.com/world/2015/jan/12/-sp-charlie-hebdo-attackers-kids-france-radicalised-paris> [accessed 23 February 2015].

the *Légion d'honneur*.[2] On 20 January, he was duly awarded French nationality in a public ceremony at the Ministry for the Interior. The ceremony was conducted by the Prime Minister, Manuel Valls, and the Interior Minister, Bernard Cazeneuve, while several other government ministers were in the audience, seated alongside representatives of the major religions and, somewhat ironically, representatives of the associations that had fought to help Bathily remain in France when threatened with expulsion several years previously.

Bathily's story reflects the complexity of sub-Saharan African immigration to France: at the age of 15, he left his mother in Mali to live with his father who had long been based in Paris; at the end of his studies, he was faced with an 'obligation de quitter le territoire' but with the aid of some of his former teachers, part of the *Réseau Éducation sans frontières*, he was able to gain a *titre de séjour* that had been renewed annually until the events of 9 January 2015. Valls and Cazeneuve both lauded the young man's bravery, and the Interior Minister attempted, somewhat implausibly, to divorce his courageous acts from the decision to grant him citizenship. As *Le Monde*'s reporter noted:

> Faut-il croire le ministre de l'intérieur lorsqu'il lui lance un « vous auriez été naturalisé, car la citoyenneté française n'est pas réservée aux braves » ? Les données chiffrées ne plaident pas vraiment pour les paroles ministérielles, puisque seuls 57 610 personnes ont obtenu la nationalité française par décret en 2014.[3]

The journalist goes on to note, however, that the trend in recent years has been towards greater numbers of immigrants being granted French nationality. Indeed, Cazeneuve declared that he had 'relancé le processus de naturalisation, car c'est une chance pour notre pays' and went on to reminisce about his father, 'instituteur de la République', who had brought children of different religions together in the classroom to forge them into French citizens, while Valls reminded the audience of his own itinerary, as the Spanish-born son of immigrants to France. The moral of these stories was self-evident: the Republican model of integration was still very much operative.

What do the starkly contrasting stories of these two young men, Amedy Coulibaly and Lassana Bathily, tell us about the position of black people in contemporary France? In many ways, Coulibaly is the type of nightmare figure

---

2. See 'Lassana Bathily, héros de la prise d'otages de Vincennes, bientôt naturalisé', *Le Monde*, 15 January 2015: < http://www.lemonde.fr/societe/article/2015/01/15/lassana-bathily-heros-de-la-prise-d-otages-de-vincennes-bientot-naturalise_4557248_3224.html> [accessed 23 February 2015].

3. See Maryline Baumard, 'Lassana Bathily, "héros" du supermarché cacher, naturalisé français', *Le Monde*, 20 January 2015: < http://www.lemonde.fr/societe/article/2015/01/20/lassana-bathily-heros-du-supermarche-casher-naturalise-francais_4560032_3224.html> [accessed 23 February 2015].

who not only fuels the perpetually outraged and anxious imagination of *Le Figaro* and other right-wing sources but is also at the heart of a more generalized fear of the non-white, Muslim other who menaces an idealized secular notion of the Republic. Bathily's case offers an obvious counterbalance to such fears. As Valls's words had stressed, yesterday's *sans-papiers* could be today's Republican hero: the black African Muslim immigrant can serve the Republic and become French.

This article aims to demonstrate that this duality in the perception of black people in France has a long history but it has taken on new forms and gained a new urgency over the past thirty years. The notion of a 'France arabe' has long had political and cultural currency – and was clearly at the heart of *Le Figaro magazine*'s alarmist front cover back in 1985[4] – but that of 'la France noire' is still relatively new. The article will thus explore why 'Black France' has now become a common popular and critical term. In addition, it will examine some of the main arguments that have come to underpin discussion of 'black' questions in France, exploring the parameters of the 'black debate' over the past decade or so and the ways it which has been intertwined with the wider 'postcolonial debate'. Finally, the article will examine a handful of key figures who might be seen to represent different facets of this emerging 'France noire'.

The history of 'Black France': friends and enemies

At the end of the First World War, perhaps the best-known and most respected black man in France was Blaise Diagne, the Senegalese representative in the *Chambre des députés*. The first black African to be elected to this role, he was initially feared by the colonial administration as a threat to French authority in the colonies: however, although he pushed for greater rights for the small number of Senegalese who enjoyed the status of French *citoyens* as inhabitants of the *quatre communes*, Diagne was no anti-colonial revolutionary. He soon proved himself a loyal servant of France, not least when, in January 1918, he accepted an invitation from Clemenceau, desperate for the extra troops that might finally bring the war to a successful conclusion while limiting the loss of further French lives, to lead a recruitment tour in French West Africa.

If the First World War served as a crucible in which the likes of Diagne and thousands of African recruits could prove their loyalty to France, then the conflict also sowed the seeds of a radical anti-colonialism that would eventually gain momentum in the aftermath of the second world conflict. In the mid-1920s, the figurehead of black anti-colonial thought and activism was Lamine Senghor, a former *tirailleur sénégalais*, who had received the *croix de guerre* for his heroism during the war. Senghor first emerged as an activist within the

---

4. 'Dossier immigration: serons-nous encore français dans 30 ans?', *Le Figaro magazine*, 26 October 1985.

Union intercoloniale, an organization created by the French Communist Party to group together anti-colonial activists from across the empire. Then, in 1926, he created France's first genuinely popular black movement, the *Comité de Défense de la Race Nègre* (CDRN), drawn largely from the small working-class black communities in the ports and major towns across the country. It was in his capacity as President of the CDRN that he was invited to deliver a speech at the inaugural congress of the League against Imperialism in Brussels in February 1927.[5] For the French anti-communist right, Lamine Senghor became living proof that the Soviet Union would seek to bring down France and its empire through an alliance with its colonial subjects.[6]

It is important not to over-simplify the parallels between the interwar years and the present: one can be loyal to France without believing in the values of a long defunct empire, while the *bête noire* of communism, which saw black and white activists work together, has today been replaced by a perceived non-white Islamic fundamentalist threat. However, one does not need to agree entirely with the authors of a recent volume who declare that *Les Années 30 sont de retour* to identify similar patterns at work today to those that operated in the interwar period through which black subjects are deemed either loyal or hostile to the Republic.[7] Within this binary logic, Blaise Diagne can be shown to have proved his loyalty in France's hour of need while Lamine Senghor turned on the nation he had served, acting on behalf of a foreign power. As is so often the case with minority groups, any form of dissent or opposition to the status quo can be mobilized as grounds to undermine the individual's very right to be considered French.

Black people in France do not need to be an Amedy Coulibaly to have their loyalty to France questioned. For instance, in the early stages of her career, the French novelist Marie NDiaye always insisted that she was simply a writer, not a black writer: her Senegalese father had played no real role in her life and she had grown up embedded in white metropolitan French culture. In an August 2009 interview given by NDiaye to *Les Inrockuptibles*, she criticised the Sarkozy government's attempts to impose a restricted notion of French identity through its much-derided 'grand débat sur l'identité nationale' (she declared the France promoted by Sarkozy to be 'monstrueuse'). When NDiaye was awarded the

---

5.   For an account of Senghor's career and his relationship with Diagne, see David Murphy, 'Defending the "Negro Race": Lamine Senghor and Black Internationalism in Interwar France', *French Cultural Studies*, 24:2 (2013), 161–73.

6.   See, in particular, the polemical tract by Gustave Gautherot, *Le Bolchévisme aux colonies et l'impérialisme rouge* (Paris: Redier, 1930).

7.   Renaud Dély, Pascal Blanchard, Claude Askolovitch and Yvan Gastaut, *Les Années 30 sont de retour: petite leçon d'histoire pour comprendre les crises du présent* (Paris: Flammarion, 2014).

Prix Goncourt in November 2009, the *Inrockuptibles* interview was unearthed and the UMP deputy for Seine-Saint-Denis, Éric Raoult declared that 'Les prises de position de Marie Ndiaye sont inacceptables. [...] Une personnalité qui défend les couleurs littéraires de la France se doit de faire preuve d'un certain respect à l'égard de nos institutions.'[8] The warning could not have been clearer: NDiaye's Frenchness was deemed to be dependent on an uncritical acceptance of a perceived status quo.

The rise of black studies *à la française*

Over the past five or six years, a wide range of academic and more popular texts, as well as wider cultural artefacts – from exhibitions to television series to documentary films – have sought to position what is now commonly termed 'La France noire' within a wider historical framework that extends beyond the wave of mass migration that began during the *trente glorieuses*. The history of black culture in France prior to the Second World War had long been dominated by accounts of jazz, Josephine Baker and the *vogue nègre* of the 1920s or, for those more interested in literature, the story of Aimé Césaire, Léon Damas, Léopold Senghor and the birth of Negritude in the 1930s. Many such accounts have sought, with some justification, to celebrate France's famed racial tolerance that was so clearly illustrated during the First World War when the coded racial hierarchies at work in the colonial Republic came face to face with the brutal segregationist mentality of the US army.

   Now, though, a wider and more complex history has emerged. For instance, the *beau-livre*, *La France Noire* (2011), edited by Pascal Blanchard, a leading figure in the ACHAC collective of scholars, bore the sub-title 'trois siècles de présences', promoting a historical engagement that encompasses slavery and colonialism, as well as more recent patterns of migration.[9] A few months later, a documentary film, *Noirs de France* (2012), co-directed by Blanchard (with Juan Gelas) was screened to audiences over three weeks on France 5: the film acted as a tele-visual companion to *La France noire* and its sub-title, 'de 1889 à nos jours: une histoire de France', declared a similar (if slightly less ambitious) desire

---

8.   Cited in Dominic Thomas, 'The "Marie Ndiaye Affair" or the Coming of a Postcolonial Évoluée', in *Transnational French Studies: Postcolonialism and Littérature-monde*, ed. by Alec G. Hargreaves, Charles Forsdick and David Murphy (Liverpool: Liverpool University Press, 2010), pp. 146–63 (p. 155). As Thomas notes, another black writer, Gaston Kelman, was only too happy to serve as an advisor to then Interior Minister Eric Besson on the national identity debate. Kelman's essay *Je suis noir et je n'aime pas le manioc* (Paris: Max Milo, 2003) is a fervent defence of the colour-blind Republic.

9.   Pascal Blanchard et al., *La France noire: trois siècles de présences* (Paris: La Découverte, 2011).

to give greater depth to black French history.[10] A few years earlier, Pap Ndiaye's *La Condition noire* (2008), a text primarily devoted to the contemporary situation of black people in France, dedicated a chapter to exploring 'une histoire des populations noires de France'.[11] One of the most high profile historical interventions was provided by the former footballer and now activist Lilian Thuram (who will be examined in greater detail below). As its sub-title suggests, his best-selling book *Mes étoiles noires: de Lucy à Barack Obama*, outlined a popular black history that extended across the centuries (and, indeed, millennia in the case of the prehistoric figure known as Lucy) and was transnational in reach.[12] Thuram has become a close collaborator with Blanchard and the ACHAC collective, working to promote a broad anti-racist agenda, not least through a major exhibition at the Musée du Quai Branly in late 2011–early 2012 – *Exhibitions: L'Invention du sauvage* – exploring the history of 'human zoos' in France and elsewhere in the Western world.[13]

The centenary of the First World War has witnessed a surge of both official and popular initiatives to mark the contribution of colonial, and in particular black, troops to the French cause in that conflict. To cite just a few examples, an exhibition on 'les tirailleurs sénégalais et la Grande Guerre' was launched at the Institut Français de Dakar in November 2014; a bande dessinée in the popular series, *L'Homme de l'année*, places a *tirailleur* at the heart of its story concerning the search for the unknown soldier to be interred under the Arc de triomphe in November 1920; and a television series *Frères d'armes* (directed by Rachid Bouchareb in collaboration with Pascal Blanchard) featuring fifty short portraits of colonial soldiers (many of them black) who fought for France in various wars has been screened on a number of French TV channels.[14] The material highlighted in these forums may not have been new to many scholars, but the

---

10. Pascal Blanchard and Juan Gélas, *Noirs de France, de 1889 à nos jours: une histoire de France*. DVD. (Paris: Cie des Phares et Balises, 2012).

11. Pap Ndiaye, *La Condition noire: essai sur une minorité française* (Paris: Calmann-Lévy, 2008).

12. Lilian Thuram, *Mes étoiles noires: de Lucy à Barack Obama* (Paris: Philippe Rey, 2010).

13. The exhibition ran from November 2011–June 2012: < www.quaibranly.fr/fr/programmation/expositions/expositions-passees/exhibitions.html> [accessed 23 February 2015]. For the festival catalogue, see Pascal Blanchard, Gilles Boëtsch and Nanette Jacomijn Snoep, *Exhibitions: l'invention du sauvage* (Arles: Actes Sud, 2011).

14. For details of the exhibition, see < http://www.institutfrancais-senegal.com/Tirailleurs-la-grande-guerre-a.html> [accessed 23 February 2015]. See Fred Duval, Jean-Pierre Pécau and Mr Fab, *L'Homme de l'année, 1917* (Paris: Delcourt, 2013). At the time of writing (March 2015), a DVD of *Frères d'armes* is due for imminent release; for further details, see the programme's website < www.seriefreresdarmes.com> [accessed 23 February 2015].

impact of these cultural interventions has been to create among a wider public a sense of a lost history at last being rediscovered.

When taken collectively, these works can be seen to have inaugurated a field of black studies *à la française*, one that has strong roots in the academy but that has also proven capable of reaching a much wider public. Pap Ndiaye's *La Condition noire* was a genuine media phenomenon with some of the more breathless commentators appearing to believe that the author had somehow single-handedly invented black studies in France, ignoring previous work by both French and Anglophone scholars. Although written in a relatively accessible style, Ndiaye's book was a thorough historical-sociological study, full of statistics and it constituted an unlikely non-fiction best seller, which has already gone through several editions. In the wake of Ndiaye's book, texts such as those by Blanchard and Thuram also enjoyed popular and critical success. Indeed, Blanchard's handsomely produced volume sold out in the run-up to Christmas 2011, suggesting that the story of blackness in France had attained the level of acceptability that allowed it to be offered as a stocking filler.[15]

In many respects, the media championing of Ndiaye's volume mirrored the frenzy that had earlier surrounded the edited volume, *La Fracture coloniale* (2005), which was published shortly before the riots that rocked the poor suburbs of many French cities in October–November 2005, and was either adopted or rejected (depending on the author's political standpoint) as a useful prism through which to attempt to comprehend the events unfolding around the country.[16] Indeed, the 'black debate' that has been launched in France is inextricably bound up in the 'postcolonial debate' that emerged around 2005 and encompasses the memory of slavery, colonization and the position of 'postcolonial minorities' within the Republic. Ann Laura Stoler summarizes this debate in the following terms:

> Colonialism and empire now appear as central threads in the [French] nation's unraveling republican fabric. There is intense disagreement about how they figure, whether a focus on the 'colonial continuum' strengthens urgent demands for social

---

15. Blanchard had, ten years earlier, published a very similar *beau-livre* (with Eric Deroo and Gilles Manceron), entitled *Le Paris noir* (Paris: Hazan, 2001), which did not enjoy the same level of popular success. That *La France noire* was so commercially successful should not be attributed solely to its intrinsic qualities but rather to the propitious conditions it enjoyed at the time of its publication.

16. *La Fracture coloniale: la société française au prisme de l'héritage colonial*, ed. by Pascal Blanchard, Nicolas Bancel and Sandrine Lemaire (Paris: La Découverte, 2005). For a discussion of the role of this volume in the emergence of a postcolonial debate in France, see Charles Forsdick and David Murphy, 'Situating Francophone Postcolonial Thought', in *Postcolonial Thought in the French-speaking World*, ed. by Forsdick and Murphy (Liverpool: Liverpool University Press, 2009), pp. 1–27.

equity or is an irrelevant distraction from them, whether repentance and guilt have shaped politics or politics has replaced good scholarship. Some would argue that the Republic and Empire are now difficult to view as mutually exclusive categories.[17]

Stoler herself is less interested in such questions than in what she refers to as 'the political, personal and scholarly dispositions that have made the racial co-ordinates of empire and the racial epistemics of governance so faintly legible to French histories of the present'.[18] It is obvious that, for many scholars, race and the French republic are now on the research agenda in ways that would have seemed unimaginable three decades ago.

If postcolonial studies in France became an acknowledged feature of academic and public discourse in 2005, then it is no coincidence that the same year also witnessed the creation of *Le Conseil Représentatif des Associations Noires* (CRAN), at first under the presidency of Patrick Lozès and, since 2011, under Louis-Georges Tin: the passing of this role from a *Béninois* to a *Martiniquais* illustrating the primarily pan-African nature of black groups in France (although this is not to deny the existence of important differences in the (self-)perception of black Africans and Antilleans, as will be explored further below). CRAN has been a vocal and some would say divisive presence in public debate over the past decade, campaigning against racial discrimination, demanding greater ethnic representation in French public life and, perhaps most controversially, promoting a debate on reparations for slavery. CRAN has given a voice to black issues in a more sustained way than would have been imaginable in 1985 but its very existence has for some in France acted as proof of the rise of an American-style identity politics, whose alleged communitarianism is a threat to the universal Republic.

At the same time, the encounter between black studies and French studies has led to the creation of a distinct area of study in the Anglophone world, not least in North America. Dominic Thomas's *Black France* (2007), which was published a year before Pap Ndiaye's best seller in France, was a landmark work that brought together the different strands of this emerging field of inquiry in a text that examined different cultural forms, contexts and historical periods.[19] 'Black France' has now become a clearly identifiable academic area of study: in 2012, an edited volume with the dual-language title, *Black France/La France*

---

17. Ann Laura Stoler, 'Colonial Aphasia: Race and Disabled Histories in France', *Public Culture*, 23:1 (2011), 121–56 (pp. 136–37).

18. Stoler, 'Colonial Aphasia', p. 122.

19. Dominic Thomas, *Black France: Colonialism, Immigration and Transnationalism* (Bloomington, IN: Indiana University Press, 2007). Thomas has further developed his reflections in this area in subsequent works: *Africa and France: Postcolonial Cultures, Migration and Racism* (Bloomington, IN: Indiana University Press, 2013); *Racial Advocacy in France* (*French Cultural Studies*, 24:2 (2013)) .

noire was published by three distinguished North American scholars and new courses have sprung up bearing this label (I teach one myself at the University of Stirling).[20] Notions such as 'Afropean literature' have also become prominent within the academy and have offered new transnational frameworks within which to situate black writing produced in France.[21] As was indicated above, discussions of 'Black France' are often conducted within the wider context of discussions of a postcolonial France, or even of a 'Racial France' to use the term adopted in the title of a 2011 special issue of *Public Culture*.[22]

Talk of the emergence of a new field can serve to occlude the existence of earlier work already engaging with such issues and there are countless books and special issues of journals that one could cite from the 1980s, 1990s and 2000s that were already committed to exploration of the black presence in France.[23] However, as was indicated above, it is no exaggeration to state that, broadly speaking, the notion of 'La France noire' has until recently seemed less of a social or critical given than that of 'La France arabe': for instance, Alec Hargreaves and Mark McKinney's groundbreaking edited volume, *Post-Colonial Cultures in France* (1997) contains a chapter on the latter topic but no separate chapter on Black France.[24] This is largely explained by demographics – there are far more 'Arabes' in France than there are black people – which has given greater visibility to North African culture but has also given rise to more pronounced fears regarding a Muslim takeover of France (a fear so clearly exploited by Michel Houellebecq in his latest novel, *Soumission*). Black people may predominantly have been viewed at various times in modern French history as objects of fear, laughter, contempt or even admiration for their physical or

20. See *Black France/France Noire: The History and Politics of Blackness*, ed. by Trica Danielle Keaton, T. Denean Sharpley-Whiting and Tyler Stovall (Durham, NC: Duke University Press, 2012). Another important edited volume in the field is *Frenchness and the African Diaspora: Identity and Uprising in Contemporary France*, ed. by Charles Tshimanga, Didier Gondola and Peter J. Bloom (Bloomington: Indiana University Press, 2009).

21. See Sabrina Brancato, 'Afro-European Literature(s): A New Discursive Category?', *Research in African Literatures*, 39:3 (2008), 1–13; and *Francophone Afropean Literatures*, ed. by Nicki Hitchcott and Dominic Thomas (Liverpool: Liverpool University Press, 2014).

22. *Racial France*, ed. by Janet Roitman (*Public Culture*, 23:1 (2011)).

23. See, for example, Philippe Dewitte, *Les Mouvements nègres en France, 1919–39* (Paris: L'Harmattan, 1985); Tracy Denean Sharpley-Whiting, *Black Venus: Sexualized Savages, Primal Fears, and Primitive Narratives in French* (Durham, NC: Duke University Press, 1999); *Black Paris*, ed. by Sam Haigh and Nicki Hitchcott (*Journal of Romance Studies*, 5:3 (2005)).

24. See David A. McMurray, 'La France arabe', in *Post-Colonial Cultures in France*, ed. by Alec G. Hargreaves and Mark McKinney (London and New York: Routledge, 1997), pp. 26–39.

sensual qualities but they have rarely induced the sense of existential panic that is reserved for 'les Arabes'. The case of Amedy Coulibaly and the authors of similarly violent anti-Semitic crimes – most notably, the brutal torture and murder of Ilan Halimi by a gang led by French Ivorian Youssouf Fofana in 2006 – has troubled the more benign perception of the black community, and those fears that have arisen have been focused primarily on (Muslim) sub-Saharan Africans. The Antillean population in France, which is largely Christian and/or secular Republican, is widely perceived to be far more 'integrated' than its often Muslim African counterparts. In addition, the former are all French citizens who have not generally had to struggle for acceptance within metropolitan France to the same degree as persons of sub-Saharan origin, who even when born in France are perceived to be 'foreign'. Whether the broad pan-Africanist identity that is exemplified by CRAN will survive the spread of such polarized perceptions remains to be seen.

The current projection of an identity broadly defined as that of a 'Black France' is undoubtedly, in part, a response to the marginalization of black people in France and to the thoughtless categorization of all young people in the *banlieues* as undifferentiated *jeunes issus de l'immigration*. I would argue, however, that the emergence of the notion of a 'Black France' has far more to do with the growing self-awareness and self-confidence of people of colour in France than with the majority population's fears about black people. Rather than attempting an exhaustive overview of the different areas of French culture in which black questions have been to the fore in recent times – sport, music, cinema, politics, media representations –, the remainder of this article will instead focus on two prominent black individuals in France whose writings and/or actions have placed them at the centre of debates on this emerging Black France: Christiane Taubira and Lilian Thuram.

Christiane Taubira: politics, race, memory

The French parliamentary deputy for Guyana, Christiane Taubira, is arguably the person of colour who has enjoyed the greatest political power and authority in the entire Fifth Republic. She was appointed *Garde des Sceaux* at the beginning of the 2012 parliament and, as will be explored below, has in this role been charged with piloting through the *Assemblée nationale* some of the most controversial of François Hollande's policies. First elected to parliament in 1993, she came to national prominence in 2001 when she played a central role in the passing of the *loi tendant à la reconnaissance de la traite et de l'esclavage en tant que crime contre l'humanité*, which has widely become known as the *loi Taubira*. A year later, she was the candidate chosen by the *Parti radical de gauche* to stand in the Presidential elections, winning 2.32% of the vote (just over 660,000 votes).

The passing of the *loi Taubira* was intended to mark a Republican consensus around the history of slavery, signalling recognition of the past suffering endured by current French citizens in the Caribbean DOMs: that is, this was primarily a gesture towards a group *within* the contemporary nation. However, in the decade since this legislation was passed, it has become all too obvious that no such Republican consensus exists. Instead, the *loi Taubira* inspired right-wing politicians and colonial nostalgics to promote similar legislation celebrating France's colonial past, which led to the *loi du 23 février 2005*, whose infamous fourth clause stated that: 'Les programmes scolaires reconnaissent en particulier le rôle positif de la présence française outre-mer, notamment en Afrique du Nord et accordent à l'histoire et aux sacrifices des combattants de l'armée française issus de ces territoires la place éminente à laquelle ils ont droit'. For their part, French historians have decried the interference of legislators in the recording, interpretation and teaching of history from whatever political perspective.[25]

Taubira's activism on issues of racial history has made her a figure of hate for many on the right in France. This became evident early in her tenure as *Garde des Sceaux* when she was at the forefront of the Ayrault government's drive to introduce legislation to legalize gay marriage. It was striking that the virulent right-wing Christian opposition to the bill regularly veered off into barely concealed racist slurs as is illustrated by three separate incidents in November 2013 at the height of the debate: a 12-year-old boy taunted her with a banana at a demonstration against the bill; shortly afterwards, Anne-Sophie Leclere, a member of Marine Le Pen's National Front party, created a photo-montage showing Taubira alongside a baby monkey (with the captions 'À 18 mois' and 'Maintenant') which was posted on her Facebook page; finally, at the end of the month, the extreme right-wing magazine, *Minute*, placed a photo of Taubira on its front cover alongside the headline: 'Maligne comme un singe, Taubira retrouve la banane'.[26] That Taubira's actions in support of legislation with no connection whatsoever to questions of race should elicit such an openly racist response is evidence that, for a certain segment of the majority French population, the colour of her skin disqualified her from high office. Over the past three years, she has thus come to act as a symbol of French diversity and equality while at the same time suffering the type of racist abuse that is an absolute denial of Republican principles of equality.

---

25. In a recent article, Charles Forsdick explores the ways in which certain French port cities have sought to commemorate their historical involvement in the slave trade. See 'Monuments, Memorials, Museums: Slavery Commemoration and the Search for Alternative Archival Spaces', *Francosphères*, 3:1 (2014), 81–98.

26. A casual Internet search in preparation for this article revealed a whole host of similarly racist imagery aimed at Taubira.

Lilian Thuram: diversity and integration

The multiracial French football team that won the 1998 World Cup were immediately heralded as symbols of the successful integration of France's postcolonial minorities. Subsequent events – from the electoral success of Jean-Marie Le Pen in 2002 to the suburban riots of 2005, through the harshly anti-immigrant tone of President Nicolas Sarkozy's national identity debates to the tragedy of the *Charlie Hebdo* massacres – have underlined the prematurely celebratory nature of this initial response.[27] It is in this troubled context that the former player Lilian Thuram has decided to use his status as an icon of the 1998 team to become a public figure who regularly speaks out on issues of race, identity and memory.[28] Thuram was born in Guadeloupe, but his family moved to mainland France in 1981, and settled in the Parisian suburb of Bois-Colombes. He was part of the most successful generation of French footballers, and he still holds the record number of appearances (142) for the French national team. Thuram thus brings a huge amount of symbolic capital with him into his chosen post-football role as a public figure seeking to combat racism.

Thuram's numerous interventions on issues of race have over the past decade been marked by two key features: firstly, there is a clear rejection of the notion of integration, for he consistently stresses 'le droit à la différence' which is a deeply problematic concept in the context of the universal French republic; secondly, he makes consistent use of what Mireille Rosello has identified as a 'tactical universalism', that is an appeal to the universal values of the Republic to defend minority rights.[29] For example, in a 2010 interview, Thuram dismissed Sarkozy's national identity debate as follows:

> Je ne comprends pas ce questionnement sur l'identité nationale alors qu'elle est inscrite sur tous les frontons de mairie: Liberté, Égalité, Fraternité. Ensuite, il y a l'identité des Français, ce qui est différent. Chaque personne a sa propre identité qu'il construit chaque jour et on ne peut pas gommer ses identités dans une tentation jacobine.[30]

---

27. The best book on the relationship between football and the postcolonial is Laurent Dubois, *Soccer Empire: The World Cup and the Future of France* (Los Angeles: University of California Press, 2011).

28. For a more sustained analysis of Thuram's intervention on race, see my article, 'When Symbols Start to Speak: Lilian Thuram and the French Identity Debates', *Moving Worlds: A Journal of Transcultural Writings*, 12:1 (2012), 19–28.

29. Mireille Rosello, 'Tactical Universalism and New Multiculturalist Claims in Postcolonial France', in *Francophone Postcolonial Studies: A Critical Introduction*, ed. by Charles Forsdick and David Murphy (London: Arnold, 2003), pp. 135–44.

30. Lilian Thuram, 'Chacun de nous a sa façon de vivre la France', in 'Où en est la France d'outre-mer', *Le Monde*, hors-série, January–February 2010, 7–9 (p. 8).

In his 2004 autobiography, Thuram had already reflected on the 1998 World Cup and how it had been interpreted by politicians and the media.[31] For Thuram, the 1998 victory had been about the celebration of France's diversity not the successful neutralization of that difference via a conception of integration that he rejected. The victory in 1998 was thus symbolic for Thuram precisely because it promised an alternative model for national identity, one that was not based on notions of integration.

In 2008, the year in which he retired as a professional footballer, Thuram established the *Fondation Lilian Thuram* whose motto is 'l'Éducation contre le racisme'.[32] If star footballers from Barcelona (Thuram's final club) constitute the public-friendly face of the Foundation, the website clearly indicates that the educational dimension of the project is led by a team of prominent researchers. The world-renowned paleoanthropologist Yves Coppens – who identified, in Ethiopia, the fossilized remains of 'Lucy' as the oldest example of human life on earth – is just one member of the eleven-strong scientific committee of the Foundation, alongside other prominent figures such as Pascal Blanchard, Michel Wieviorka, the renowned sociologist, and Tzvetan Todorov, the literary critic and theorist of race and alterity. If his *comité scientifique* provide the reasoned arguments and in-depth knowledge that he lacks, it is Thuram's celebrity and in many ways his aura of authenticity, as a representative from a working-class ethnic minority background, someone who has engaged with race and identity in real life rather than solely in textbooks, that provides the conduit for these ideas to be debated in a popular public forum.

In January 2010, Thuram published *Mes étoiles noires: de Lucy à Barack Obama*, and embarked on a round of print and broadcast media interviews that confirmed his transition from sportsman to public figure. (Although *Mes étoiles noires* is his best-known intervention on race, Thuram has consistently contributed to public debate on these issues in various ways. He is a regular *préfacier* to texts touching on race – for example, see his preface to Thomté Ryam's *Banlieue noire* – and has contributed to a number of manifestos on race and multiculturalism, including an 'Appel pour une République multiculturelle et postraciale' in 2010, and a *Manifeste pour l'égalité* in 2012.[33]) As its title indicates (the reference to 'black stars' deliberately echoing Marcus Garvey),

31. Lilian Thuram, *Le 8 juillet 1998* (Paris: Anne Carrière, 2004).

32. Thuram's website can be accessed at: < www.thuram.org >.

33. Lilian Thuram et al., *Appel pour une République multiculturelle et postraciale*. Published as supplement to *Respect Mag: urbain, social et métissé*, 24 (January–March 2010). *Manifeste pour l'égalité*, ed. by Lilian Thuram (Paris: Autrement, 2012). For analysis of the former text, see my article, 'The Postcolonial Manifesto: partisanship, criticism and the performance of change', in *Transnational French Studies*, ed. by Hargreaves, Forsdick and Murphy, pp. 67–86.

the book is an eclectic series of portraits of his 'black heroes', which stretches from the Lucy discovered by Yves Coppens to the current US president. As with his website, the primary impulse behind his book is educational. In the introduction, he reflects on the fact that the first time he heard about black people in school was when the class studied slavery. The study of slavery is of course crucial but what upset Thuram was that there was not a single positive role model for black children, and it is this absence that his book seeks to address. If his alternative Pantheon contains figures around whom a genuine Republican consensus might be found such as the Chevalier de Saint Georges, Nelson Mandela or Aimé Césaire, there are other more troublesome figures for a Republican history of the French nation: from the Haitian revolutionaries, Toussaint Louverture and Jean-Jacques Dessalines, to those arch-critics of French (neo-)colonialism, Frantz Fanon and Mongo Beti. The task of changing French society is cast in explicitly Fanonian terms, which involves the deconstruction of the very ways in which people conceive of race: 'l'âme noire, le peuple noir, la pensée noire n'existent pas plus que l'âme blanche, le peuple blanc ou la pensée blanche'.[34] He pre-empts and rejects the dreaded and inevitable charge that he is engaging in 'communitarianism', shattering the unity of the universal Republic by promoting communal minority identities: to create a truly universal Republic, it is necessary to bring an end to racialized forms of thought and perception: 'Seul le changement de nos imaginaires peut nous rapprocher et faire tomber nos barrières culturelles' (p. 9). When one considers that then French President Nicolas Sarkozy had visited the Senegalese capital, Dakar, shortly after his election in 2007 to claim that Africa was a continent outside of history, one can clearly see that a colonial-era racial *imaginaire* did not simply disappear with the formal collapse of empire.[35] Under Hollande, there have been clear attempts to row back from Sarkozy's racial and colonialist excesses but the open racism towards Christiane Taubira that was mentioned above illustrates that racialized thought has not disappeared with the passage of the presidency from the right to the socialists.

Conclusion

In the 2011 film, *Intouchables* (directed by Eric Toledano/Olivier Nakache), Omar Sy, a black French actor of Senegalese origin, plays Driss, an unemployed young *banlieusard* who forms an unlikely odd-couple friendship with the rich paraplegic man he is hired to care for. The film was a runaway box office success,

---

34. Thuram, *Mes étoiles noires*, p. 9.
35. Sarkozy's speech in July 2007 provoked an angry response from many African artists and intellectuals. To cite just two examples, see *L'Afrique de Sarkozy: un déni d'histoire*, ed. by Jean-Pierre Chrétien (Paris: Karthala, 2008), and Makhily Gassama, *L'Afrique répond à Sarkozy: contre le discours de Dakar* (Paris: Philippe Rey, 2008).

attracting a remarkable audience of 19 million in France alone. The film was adored by many critics who argued that the film finally allowed a predominantly white French audience to embrace a black French character, while others dismissed it as a rehashing of tired racial clichés.

At the other end of the comic spectrum lies Dieudonné M'Bala M'Bala who, over the past decade, has arguably become the most notorious black figure in France. Born to a white French mother and a Cameroonian father, he grew up in a relatively privileged middle-class household in the suburbs of Paris. Originally a figure broadly of the left, he has gradually veered towards a far right, anti-Semitic agenda that manages to embrace aspects of a Front National agenda while simultaneously espousing the hate-filled ideas of a minority of the black community towards Israel and Jewish people more generally. In typically provocative fashion, he commented on Facebook shortly after the terror attacks of January 2015 that 'Je me sens Charlie Coulibaly', setting his face against the overwhelming expression of solidarity towards the victims, instead expressing a grimly comic solidarity with Amedy Coulibaly.

I would argue that these final two case studies encapsulate the ambivalence surrounding the position of black people in contemporary France. Depending on one's point of view, *Intouchables* invites us to laugh with, or at, the black male *banlieusard*. However, perhaps most significantly, it also signifies the acceptance of black characters within a longstanding, popular French comic tradition. As for Dieudonné, he may appear to some in France as the bastard offspring of the light entertainment wings of ISIS/FN but what is most striking from my perspective here is that his audience is so racially mixed; those who claim most vocally that his inverted Nazi salute, the *quenelle*, is merely an anti-Establishment gesture are often young white French people who situate themselves within an anarchic tradition of non-conformism that in many respects shares the ethos that informs *Charlie Hebdo*. *Intouchables* and Dieudonné are quite clearly products of French culture and tradition, but equally they ask questions of that culture that would not have been asked 30 years ago. That is as it should be, for the French nation of three decades ago is, by its very nature, not the same as the French nation in 2015, though contrary to *Le Figaro's* alarmism this does not of course mean that it is no longer French.

Nottingham French Studies 54.3 (2015): 253–268
DOI: 10.3366/nfs.2015.0125
© University of Nottingham
www.euppublishing.com/journal/nfs

HOW FRENCH IS 'FRENCH' SPORT?

PHILIP DINE

Introduction

Scholarship on modern games and the construction of identity has tended to foreground representations of the nation, arguing that 'Sporting competition [...] provides the primary expression of imagined communities; the nation becoming more "real" in the domain of sport.'[1] This reflects the simultaneous rise of athletic sports and the consolidation of the nation-state, together with industrialization and urbanization. In France, as elsewhere in Western Europe, modernization thus went hand-in-hand with 'sportization'. The mass literacy which underpinned this process made possible the expression of sport-inflected nationalist sentiment in the later nineteenth and early twentieth centuries; while the burgeoning popular press itself played a key role in the establishment of athletic competition as an enduring vehicle for national self-images. The launch in 1903 of the Tour de France cycle race epitomizes this linkage, occurring as it did against the backdrop of the Dreyfus Affair and as a by-product of the ensuing circulation war between rival sports papers. The event was the brainchild of Henri Desgrange, editor of *L'Auto*, which was itself established by the automobile manufacturer, and leading anti-*Dreyfusard*, Baron Jules-Albert de Dion specifically to compete with Pierre Giffard's *Le Vélo*, the pioneering journal which had supported Captain Alfred Dreyfus both before and after his notoriously flawed conviction for treason. This highly politicized invention of a French tradition reminds us that, from the outset, sporting nationalism has had at least as much to do with alterity as with identity, and hence with variously threatening (non-national) Others, typically contrasted with an ethnically imagined (national) Self.

In the case of the Tour de France, the allegedly hostile Jewishness of Dreyfus paved the way for assorted oppositions on the country's roads, as cyclists from across continental Europe competed at the pinnacle of the single standardized sport which was indisputably French in origin.[2] Over the years, the race became synonymous with the nation, functioning as a mobile celebration of unity in

1. Joseph Maguire and Jason Tuck, 'Global Sports and Patriot Games: Rugby Union and National Identity in a United Sporting Kingdom since 1945', in *Sporting Nationalisms: Identity, Ethnicity, Immigration and Assimilation*, ed. by Mike Cronin and David Mayall (London: Frank Cass, 1998), pp. 103–26 (p. 106).

2. Maarten Van Bottenburg, *Global Games*, transl. by Beverley Jackson (Urbana: University of Illinois Press, 2001), p. 45.

diversity, and constituting an authentic *lieu de mémoire*.[3] However, even this archetypal manifestation of sporting specificity has been challenged by the forces of globalization, with its 1985 and 1986 editions together marking a watershed. The 1985 race was won by the veteran Bernard Hinault, in what was both his fifth triumph and the climax of a decade of French dominance. Thirty years on, no home-produced rider has managed to emulate Hinault's victory. Just as significantly, Greg LeMond's win in 1986, the first by a non-European competitor, launched a new era of internationalism, including an American engagement with the race which would culminate, competitively and commercially, in the seven straight victories (1999–2005) recorded by the now disgraced Lance Armstrong. Since Armstrong's departure, three Spaniards, two Britons, an Italian, a Luxembourger and even an Australian have won the Tour, but still no Frenchman, although the second and third places achieved by Jean-Christophe Péraud and Thibaut Pinot in 2014 bode well for the race as a renewed competitive opportunity, as well as a particularly cherished, and proportionately lucrative, heritage industry.

So much for a quintessentially French event which has fittingly been characterized as a 'pre-modern contest in a post-modern context'.[4] But how have other sports responded to the challenges of globalization, and also to the opportunities of an increasingly multicultural society? Two case studies are offered here in which a distinctive national model may be seen to have been exposed to powerful transnational forces between 1985 and 2015, a period which also corresponds to sport's digital age. Several activities potentially suggest themselves for discussion: basketball, as an obvious American import, additionally noteworthy for France's silver medal at the 2000 (Sydney) Olympics, as well as for the subsequent recruitment by the National Basketball Association (NBA) of leading (and mainly black) French players; handball, especially given the prominence of the 1995 and 2001 World Championship-winning sides captained by Jackson Richardson (from La Réunion); and even fencing, in which the five Olympic medals, including two golds, won by Laura Flessel-Colovic (from Guadeloupe), between 1996 and 2004, make her France's leading female Olympian. However, the sports targeted here are football and athletics, the most visibly international of modern games, as highlighted by their quadrennial showcases: the World Cup and the Olympic Games. The resulting case studies are intended to suggest some of the ways in which the state, the media and the relevant federations have responded to the multiple challenges of the corporate-financed and electronically mediated

---

3. Georges Vigarello, 'Le Tour de France', in *Les Lieux de Mémoire: Tome III, Les France – traditions*, ed. by Pierre Nora (Paris: Gallimard, 1992), pp. 884–925.

4. Hugh Dauncey and Geoff Hare, 'The Tour de France: A Pre-Modern Contest in a Post-Modern Context', *International Journal of the History of Sport*, 20:2 (2003), 1–29.

'global sporting system'.[5] There is an irony here in that the two mega-events which nowadays 'are the preeminent symbol of the global character of sport'[6] both originated in France: Pierre de Coubertin's Olympic Games in 1896; and Jules Rimet's World Cup in 1930. To which we might add Henri Desgrange's 1903 creation of the Tour de France, often regarded as the world's third biggest sporting event. As we explore the impact of globalization in more recent years, it is helpful to bear in mind this pivotal contribution to the internationalization of modern games.

French football, 1985–2015: a hesitation waltz with postcolonial ethnicity

One obvious strategy for responding to the challenges of globalization is to embrace the human potential of any society marked by a history of immigration. Sport in France is consequently not unusual in having a strong representation of elite practitioners of migrant heritage. As John Bale and Mike Cronin, working in the British context, have contended: 'From a macro-perspective we would argue that sport *per se* is an eminently postcolonial phenomenon.'[7] In the French case, the outstanding example of multicultural fusion remains the triumph of *Les Bleus* at the 1998 football World Cup. Much has been written about the on-field exploits and off-field symbolism of the so-called *black-blanc-beur* side, and almost as much about its fall from grace in subsequent editions of the tournament, including first-round exits in 2002 and 2010; not to mention the extraordinary circumstances of defeat in the 2006 final, which will forever be remembered for Zinedine Zidane's valedictory *coup de boule*. Given this remarkable history, the French team's solid all-round performance in the 2014 competition constituted something of a return to sporting normality. In symbolic terms, and with the benefit of hindsight, it is clear that the significance of France's victory as host nation in 1998 – itself not actually an infrequent occurrence, as England's own single win in 1966 reminds us – was widely overestimated. Such a triumph would have generated popular enthusiasm at any time, especially considering that the World Cup is a French invention and that the trophy had never previously been won by the national side. However, this generally unexpected victory was undoubtedly perceived at the time as a defining moment for the Republic, heralding a new consensus as regards migration, ethnicity and, crucially, social inclusion.

The widespread optimism which greeted the French triumph in 1998 was not wholly a product of journalistic imagination and political wishful thinking. One of those best placed to comment was Lilian Thuram, a key member of the

---

5.   Van Bottenburg, *Global Games*, pp. 1–9.

6.   Ibid., p. 8.

7.   John Bale and Mike Cronin, 'Introduction: Sport and Postcolonialism', in *Sport and Postcolonialism*, ed. by John Bale and Mike Cronin (Oxford: Berg, 2003), pp. 1–13 (p. 4).

cup-winning side who would go on to become an incisive commentator on race relations. Looking back on the win in 2004, he commented:

> Dans l'euphorie de la victoire, j'avais l'impression que nous étions devenus le modèle parfait [...]. La plus grande richesse de cette équipe de France, c'était sa diversité culturelle. Ce jour-là, les personnes qui avaient des problèmes identitaires se trouvaient libérées de ce carcan.[8]

With the state's encouragement, the spontaneous festivity of 12 July 1998 seamlessly transitioned into the national celebration of *le quatorze juillet*. However, this political appropriation belied the competing meanings which could be placed on events both on and off the pitch. Encapsulating Thuram's own reassessment, Laurent Dubois argues:

> The victory of 1998 was not a confirmation that the reigning models of citizenship and immigration were working in France. It was a crucial opportunity to question and critique these models and to build on celebrations that provided a promising alternative. The mass communion that took place in the streets in 1998, liberating many from the shackles of their own uncertainty about their place in French society, should serve as a charter for a different way of being French.[9]

Instead, sport would frequently be appealed to in the wake of 1998 as an antidote to perceived problems of integration at the local level, while serving as an alibi for the continued national failure of political will as regards structural disadvantage and entrenched exclusion. It would not take long for frustration at this sporting smokescreen to make itself felt, appropriately back at the Stade de France stadium. The limitations of the state's moral and material investment in sport post-1998 were dramatically revealed by the pitch invasion which brought to an end the first ever match between the full national teams of France and Algeria in October 2001. As Yvan Gastaut has observed, the Algerian supporters who booed the *Marseillaise* before the match and *Les Bleus* during it, before forcing the game's abandonment, were typically French citizens of Maghrebian heritage, who seized on the occasion to highlight the continuing

---

8. Lilian Thuram, *8 juillet 1998* (Paris: Anne Carrière, 2004); cited in Yvan Gastaut, *Le Métissage par le foot: l'intégration, mais jusqu'où?* (Paris: Autrement, 2008), p. 39.

9. Laurent Dubois, *Soccer Empire: The World Cup and the Future of France* (Berkeley, CA: University of California Press, 2010), p. 169. On the legacy of 1998, see also *France and the 1998 World Cup: The National Impact of a World Sporting Event*, ed. by Geoff Hare and Hugh Dauncey (London: Frank Cass, 1999); Lindsay Sarah Krasnoff, *The Making of Les Bleus: Sport in France, 1958–2010* (Lanham, MD: Lexington Books, 2013); Cathal Kilcline, 'Playing out the Postcolonial: Football and Commemoration', in *France's Colonial Legacies: Memory, Identity and Narrative*, ed. by Fiona Barclay (Cardiff: University of Wales Press, 2013), pp. 207–26.

reality of discrimination.[10] While not as spectacular, similar demonstrations marked the French games against Morocco in November 2007 and Tunisia in October 2008, leading President Nicolas Sarkozy to summon the head of the Fédération Française de Football (FFF) to the Elysée.

With the notable exception of the Far Right, politicians of every stripe had scrambled to associate themselves with the triumph of 1998, none more so than Sarkozy's predecessor Jacques Chirac, who continued to be an astute reader of the public mood when *Les Bleus* next appeared in the World Cup final in 2006. As Dubois has observed, whatever else happened in the golden summer of 1998, 'it also represented the arrival of a global brand: Zidane'.[11] Eight years later, the star came out of retirement to lead France all the way to the tournament decider, where he put his team ahead with an idiosyncratic 'Panenka' penalty. Then, famously, Zidane was sent off in the dying minutes of extra time for head-butting the Italian defender Marco Matarazzi, who had coincidentally scored the equalizer. Once again, so much has been written about this globally iconic event that little more is needed here. However, we might usefully note Jonathan Ervine's observation that, 'Despite his expulsion, the French press was largely restrained in its criticism of Zidane and rarely sought to portray his behaviour as a symbol of his socio-ethnic origins.'[12] For his part, Chirac went significantly further at an official reception for the French team, saluting Zidane as 'un virtuose, un génie du football mondial, un homme de cœur, d'engagement, de conviction', before telling the star: 'C'est pour cela que la France vous admire et vous aime.'[13] With these words, the President of the Republic underlined Zidane's status as an embodiment of the French nation; just as Head of State Abdelaziz Bouteflika would claim the megastar for Algeria during what became a triumphal visit to his parents' homeland a few months later.[14]

Nicolas Sarkozy was to prove less sure-footed when confronted with the national side's on-field shortcomings and off-field meltdown four years later in South Africa. Now with an even stronger representation of players of migrant heritage, *Les Bleus* not only failed to perform on the pitch but very publicly rebelled against their widely criticized manager, Raymond Domenech, whom the

---

10. Gastaut, *Le Métissage par le foot*, pp. 139–43.

11. Dubois, *Soccer Empire*, p. 169.

12. Jonathan Ervine, '*Les banlieues* and *Les Bleus*: Political and Media Discourse', *French Cultural Studies*, 25:1 (2014), 70–81 (p. 74).

13. Le Monde.fr (with AFP and Reuters), 'De retour en France, les Bleus accueillis à l'Elysée et applaudis à la Concorde', *Le Monde*, 10 July 2006.

14. Yvan Gastaut, 'Le "voyage officiel" de Zinedine Zidane en Algérie en 2006 ou le retour du fils prodige', in *Les Footballeurs maghrébins de France au XXe siècle: itinéraires professionnels, identités complexes*, ed. by Sarah Clément and Yvan Gastaut (*Migrance*, 29 (2008)), 60–72.

similarly unpopular President unwisely supported with secret telephone calls at the height of the crisis.[15] The players' revolt – exemplified by Nicolas Anelka's verbal outbursts, enthusiastically reported by *L'Équipe* – encouraged politicians and intellectuals to enter the fray. Most vociferous was the neo-conservative Alain Finkielkraut, who had previously commented unfavourably on the national side's evolution from a *black-blanc-beur* team to a *black-black-black* one.[16] These remarks were made to the Israeli newspaper *Ha'aretz* in the wake of the 2005 *banlieue* riots, which had themselves been triggered in the suburb of Clichy-sous-Bois by the tragic deaths of two local youths, Zyed Benna and Bouna Traoré. They were part of a group which, for reasons which remain unclear, entered a building site while returning home from an informal football game on the pitch of a neighbouring suburb; pursued by the police, the pair were electrocuted when they tried to hide in an electrical substation. Speaking on national radio, and employing loaded vocabulary that echoed Sarkozy's own when Minister of the Interior, Finkielkraut now asserted that 'on a rêvé avec l'équipe de la génération Zidane, aujourd'hui on a plutôt envie de vomir avec la génération caillera'.[17] Sports sociologist Patrick Mignon responded incisively in *Esprit* that events in South Africa were wholly over-invested with symbolic meaning, just as had been the triumph of *Les Bleus* in Saint-Denis a dozen years earlier. In each case, the hazards of competition had given rise to a national psychodrama, with the race-based pessimism of 2010 serving as a negative mirror-image of the multicultural optimism of 1998.[18]

Ironically, France's footballing difficulties have coincided with new opportunities for players opting to compete for the nations of their familial heritage. Options of that nature are open to footballers who, because they have connections (by birth, nationality, family origins or current residence) with more than one country can choose which of these countries they want to play for internationally. The impact of this dual eligibility has been particularly marked in the case of the Algerian national side. Having secured a memorable draw against England in South Africa, *Les Fennecs* made it to the knock-out stage for the first time four years later in Brazil, only going out after extra time to eventual winners Germany, who went on to beat *Les Bleus* in the next round. Had Algeria won, the social impact, in both countries, of a clash with France in the quarter-finals of the World Cup might have been considerable. What is certain is that, in a striking example of reverse migration, the Algerian heroics in 2010 and again in 2014 were achieved by squads more than two-thirds of whom were French-born,

15.   Bruno Jeudy and Karim Nedjari, *Sarkozy côté vestiaires* (Paris: Plon, 2010), pp. 19–20.

16.   Dubois, *Soccer Empire*, p. 242.

17.   Ervine, '*Les banlieues* and *Les Bleus*', p. 76.

18.   Patrick Mignon, 'Le psychodrame du football français', *Esprit*, August–September 2010, pp. 6–22 (p. 6).

including many who had represented France at youth level. As Mustapha Kessous asked in *Le Monde*: 'L'Algérie, l'autre équipe de France?'[19] Regardless of the two countries' relative performances on the international stage, the quasi-colonial power relations at play in the decision-making of doubly eligible players remain transparent: 'Basically, if you're born in France to parents of Algerian descent and are very good – like Manchester City's Samir Nasri, Real Madrid's Karim Benzema, and arguably the greatest French player ever, Zinedine Zidane – you play for France. If you're only pretty good, you play for Algeria.'[20]

In the wake of France's South African debacle, the 'quotas' affair of 2011 embroiled Laurent Blanc, Raymond Domenech's replacement as national coach and a veteran of 1998, in another race-related crisis. The scandal involved the setting of secret quotas on the number of players of migrant heritage eligible for the French football federation's youth training programmes. In Andrew Hussey's characteristically robust formulation: 'The Blanc affair is no more or less than a debate about who is to be included in French life and who is to be excluded from it. This has the greatest impact in the *banlieues*, [...] where football is often the only escape.'[21] However, more telling than either journalistic interventions or political recriminations was the result of the 2013 FIFA Under-20 World Cup, which was won for the first time by *Les Bleuets de France*. No less concretely than Thuram and Zidane before them, the multicultural French junior side thus 'delivered several answers to the question of how racism and exclusion should be confronted. Above all, they responded by *being* France, undeniably and victoriously, branding the national consciousness with their presence in an irrefutable and profound way.'[22]

Before moving on to athletics, we may note in passing the broader transnational forces at play in French football, including the domestic league's continuing reliance on the recruitment of African players, as highlighted by the *Annual Review of the European Football Players' Labour Market*, which indicates that in 2008: 'The highest concentration of African footballers per club was recorded in France and in Belgium. This result confirms the importance of the continuity of bonds inherited from the history of territories in the geographical configuration of flows, even within the context of globalization.'[23] Conversely, increased transnational mobility has seen both top French players and some managers drawn to other European leagues, exemplified by Arsène Wenger's

---

19. Mustapha Kessous, 'L'Algérie, l'autre équipe de France, *Le Monde*, 18 June 2010.

20. Tony Ross, '"The other French team": Soccer and independence in Algeria', *Washington Post*, 6 June 2014.

21. Andrew Hussey, 'A race scandal, a fight for France's soul', *The Guardian*, 8 May 2011.

22. Dubois, *Soccer Empire*, p. 274.

23. Citation and commentary by Raffaele Poli, 'African Migrants in Asian and European Football: Hopes and Realities', *Sport in Society*, 13:6 (2010), 1001–11 (pp. 1005–6).

thirty-year tenure as manager at a distinctly francocentric Arsenal. For its part, the petrodollar-financed takeover of Paris Saint-Germain may have served to diminish the symbolic value of this not infrequently controversial club: 'Since the takeover of PSG in 2011 by Qatar Sports Investments (QSI), the focus on the local or even the national has become less important as the club has set to establish itself on the European and international stage by signing internationally known players such as Thiago Silva, Zlatan Ibrahimovic and David Beckham.'[24] These are varieties of sporting delocalization which we will see repeated in French athletics.

French athletics, 1985–2015: postcolonial performance and Americanized individualism
French athletics displays a postcolonial division of labour which has clear parallels in other national contexts, with elite performance in sprint events typically the domain of athletes of Caribbean or sub-Saharan heritage, while distance running at the highest level has long been the preserve of Maghrebian athletes. To make such an observation is, first and foremost, to draw attention to the historical coincidence of the rise (and rise) of modern sport and the rise (and fall) of the European colonial empires. The imbrication of imperialism and 'sportization' has been most extensively documented in the British context, but it is also now clear that France too sought to use sport for colonial purposes, often looking to its empire for representatives in the new international competitions which French pioneers had done so much to establish. Imperial administrators thus established patterns of recruitment that we would recognize today, particularly in athletics, as best illustrated by the Algerian-born winner of the Olympic marathon at the 1956 (Melbourne) Games, Alain Mimoun (originally Ali Mimoun Ould Kacha). This celebrated figure's standing is underlined by the fifty odd stadiums, fifteen streets and other public buildings which today bear his name and by the fulsome manner in which his remarkable contribution to French sport was duly celebrated on his death in 2013 at the age of 92.[25]

Mimoun's outstanding career reflects the extensive participation of Maghrebian competitors in distance running in the 1950s.[26] Following the accession to independence of Morocco and Tunisia in 1956, and Algeria in 1962, this athletic strength was maintained through performances such as the silver medal won by the Moroccan Rhadi Ben Abdesselam at the 1960 Olympics. In contrast, the Rome

---

24. Ervine, '*Les banlieues* and *Les Bleus*', p. 73.
25. See, for instance, Le Monde.fr (with AFP), 'Athlétisme: Alain Mimoun est mort', *Le Monde*, 28 June 2013.
26. Manuel Schotté and Carine Érard, 'Retour sur une "contribution" coloniale: le succès des coureurs nord-africains dans l'athlétisme français des années 1950', *Loisirs et société*, 29:2 (2007), 423–48.

Games were a historic low point for France, which won no gold medals at all, and only five in total, prompting an outraged General de Gaulle to embark on a state-managed transformation of sports funding and administration. Back on the track, the Tunisian runner Mohammed Gammoudi's silver medals in the 10,000m at the 1964 (Tokyo) Olympics and the 5000m at the 1972 (Munich) Games came either side of his gold medal in the latter event at Mexico City in 1968. Gammoudi, Ben Abdesselam and their compatriots thus both maintained a North African sporting tradition and pointed the way forward to the global superstars who would emerge from the 1980s onwards, such as Hassiba Boulemerka and Noureddine Morceli of Algeria, and Saïd Aouita and Hicham El Guerrouj of Morocco.

In the period 1985–2015, distance running in France has benefitted from the combined talents of athletes of Maghrebian heritage and naturalized competitors from North Africa, especially Morocco. The national records maintained by the Fédération Française d'Athlétisme (FFA) are eloquent in this regard, underlining the continuing dominance of such athletes. Current record-holders born in Morocco include Abdellah Béhar, Mustapha Essaïd, Ismaïl Sghyr and Abdellatif Meftah, the last two of whom also competed for that nation before switching to France. French-born record-holders include Mehdi Baala, who took silver in the 1500m at the 2003 World Championships and bronze at the 2008 (Beijing) Olympic Games; as well as Mahiedine Mekhissi-Benabbad who won the silver medal in the 3000m steeplechase in Beijing, and of whom we shall have more to say later. As regards sprint events, and focusing on women's athletics, a striking feature of French national teams has been the strong representation of runners from the Caribbean, with Guadeloupe-born athletes a particularly constant presence, including as current record-holders. Such elite sportswomen include Francine Landre, Christine Arron and Patricia Girard, as well as France's most celebrated female athlete, Marie-José Pérec, whose five national records have stood for two decades.[27] By revisiting her case we may usefully make some general observations about both the opportunities and the challenges of diversity for French sport.

This remarkable competitor was born in May 1968, just a few months before Colette Besson became the first Frenchwoman to win an Olympic track gold in the 400m, the event which Pérec would go on to make her own. At the same Mexico Games, Roger Bambuck, also from Guadeloupe, won a bronze medal in the 100m relay. This was the highlight of an athletic career that served as the

---

27. Record details from the relevant sections of the FFA website < http://www.athle.fr/ffa.
performance/>; supplemented by information from < http://www.lequipe.fr/base/
athletisme/records.html> and athlete profiles held by the International Association of
Athletics Federations (IAAF) < http://www.iaaf.org/home> [all accessed 27 February
2015].

springboard for another as a politician, which would see Bambuck become Minister for Youth and Sport in 1988. However, the 1968 Olympics would be globally remembered for an altogether more dramatic gesture of postcolonial political assertion, namely the black-power salutes by Tommie Smith and John Carlos at the medal ceremony for the 200m. Pérec's own experiences both on and off the track may be located somewhere between these poles of institutional accommodation and radical rejection. Cathal Kilcline has recently presented a detailed analysis of the star's representation, documenting 'how a sporting figure serves as a prism through which prevailing attitudes towards money, America, race, sexuality, and the media's role in society are reflected'.[28] World champion in 1991 and 1995, Pérec cemented her reputation as an exceptional athletic force through her gold medal in the 400m at the 1992 (Barcelona) Olympics and, especially, her double triumph in the 200m and 400m at the 1996 (Atlanta) Games.

As recounted by Kilcline, Pérec's competitive success was appropriated by the media in ways which aestheticized her performances on the track, while asserting her 'metropolitan' integration off it:

> In terms of her social ascension, Pérec traces a typically heroic narrative in leaving behind a poor childhood in the Caribbean to attain glory in major cities and mega-events. In the mid-1980s, a teenage Pérec, like many of the foremost Antillean sportspeople of recent time, left Guadeloupe for Paris and the Institut National du Sport et de l'Éducation Physique (INSEP) in the Bois de Vincennes.[29]

However, it was the racially inflected sexualization, and attendant trivialization, of her extraordinary achievements that would increasingly outrage the athlete. The most flagrant example of such coverage was L'Équipe Magazine's illustration of her 1991 World Championship win with a half-page close-up of her lycra-clad buttocks, which Pérec would very publicly condemn at the press conference called to celebrate her victory in the Olympic 400m in Barcelona the following year. Not that this dissuaded journalists at Libération from giving over the whole of their front page to a similar image to mark Pérec's historic double gold at Atlanta in 1996.[30] The athlete's long history of difficult relations with the media may readily be understood against this backdrop.

However, what had really enraged journalistic commentators in the build-up to the Atlanta Games – the first to be privately funded, most notably by the city's emblematic global brand, Coca-Cola – was Pérec's decision to leave France and

---

28. Cathal Kilcline, 'Constructing and Contesting the (Post-)national Sporting Hero: Media, Money, Mobility and Marie-José Pérec', *French Cultural Studies*, 25:1 (2014), 82–100 (p. 83).
29. Ibid., p. 85.
30. Ibid.

base herself in California as a member of the hyper-elite group of runners coached by John Smith under the 'Hudson-Smith International' (HSI) banner. As Kilcline notes: 'The acronym revealed the underlying aim of the organization – to assemble a multinational group of elite sprinters where identification with the group (and hence with the coach) would take precedence over national allegiances.'[31] By primarily committing herself to this body, rather than the FFA, Pérec not unreasonably intended to optimize her chances of success. However, this practical objective had a broader resonance as, by quite literally voting with her feet for Smith's dream of 'a post-national organization of athletic mega-events', Pérec was perceived to have betrayed not only the Olympic values championed by Pierre de Coubertin, but also traditional constructions of national cohesion in favour of personal opportunism and thus, ultimately, her own material interests.[32] Ironically, France achieved its best ever results at Atlanta, finishing fifth in the medal table with 15 gold, 7 silver and 15 bronze medals. Nevertheless, the 1996 Games, including Pérec's role in them, were widely portrayed as a nightmare vision of corporate capitalism and hegemonic Americanization.

In the wake of Atlanta, Pérec's career became something of a soap opera, as media attention focused on her alleged off-track *caprices* rather than her on-track performance, culminating in her closely monitored departure from Australia just prior to the 2000 (Sydney) Olympics. Having pulled out of a series of important competitions in the weeks leading up to the Games, the reigning champion was pursued by journalists when she arrived to prepare for her anticipated showdown with local star Cathy Freeman. Pérec would go on to allege that she was subjected to abusive treatment by the Australian press and also claimed to have been the victim of security breaches intended to harm her chances of retaining her Olympic 400m title. Unsurprisingly, her sudden decision to leave the country was perceived by many as having been prompted by fear of a looming defeat, and was widely reported as such. Although the runner did not formally retire until 2004, this episode effectively brought her competitive activity to a close, also impacting negatively on her public esteem: 'In the aftermath of her leaving Sydney, her geographic and sentimental distancing of herself from the French delegation facilitated the discarding of Pérec from the narrative of national and Olympic solidarity.'[33] In recent years, the former champion would seem to have been officially rehabilitated, through her involvement as a celebrity ambassador for the FFA, her election to the presidency of the Ligue Régionale d'Athlétisme de la Guadeloupe and, perhaps most tellingly, the use of her image on the flag flying at the entrance to the national centre for sporting excellence,

---

31. Ibid., p. 88.
32. Ibid.
33. Ibid., p. 96.

INSEP (rebranded in 2009 as the Institut National du Sport, de l'Expertise et de la Performance).[34]

Fifteen years on from the drama of Australia, 'la Guadeloupéenne' was invited by *Le Monde* to look back on her career. While not referring specifically to her Caribbean heritage, she does highlight the peculiarly intense, and even existential, combination of obsessive self-assertion and excessive public expectation which characterized her performance of both individual and collective identity on the running tracks of the world. Her comments are particularly striking for the way in which, in her final sentence, Pérec rather oddly refers to herself in the third person, effectively paraphrasing her many critics within the media:

> Après le coup de pistolet, j'étais quand même bien relâchée. Lorsque j'écoute les sportifs, je ne me reconnais pas. C'était une question de vie ou de mort pour moi. Une course pas gagnée était la fin du monde. Je voulais toutes les gagner, même les tours dans les championnats. Je ne voulais jamais être en dessous d'un certain niveau et je me prenais au sérieux. Quand on est comme ça, on se met la pression, ajoutée à celle de l'équipe de France. Nous n'étions pas nombreux et on attendait que la favorite rentre avec la médaille. Comme en plus elle n'était pas gentille avec les journalistes, ils allaient la tailler.[35]

This candid assessment of the asocial and even antisocial experience of exceptional sporting achievement, paradoxically felt most acutely by the symbolically invested national champion, may usefully be compared with a more recent case of athletic celebration combined with media condemnation: that of the frequently controversial runner, Mahiedine Mekhissi-Benabbad.

The European record-holder in the 3000m steeplechase, and a double Olympic silver medal-winner in that event in 2008 and 2012, the athlete has also made headlines beyond the sports pages. In 2011, he became embroiled in a post-race brawl with compatriot Mehdi Baala, who is also of Maghrebian heritage. More bizarrely, the runner was involved in violent incidents with official mascots at the European Championships in Barcelona in 2010 and again at Helsinki in 2012, having won the 3000m steeplechase on both occasions. He has additionally been the target of unsubstantiated allegations of doping, particularly after his unpredicted Olympic silver at Beijing in 2008. Most recently and most dramatically, he was disqualified in the 3000m steeplechase at the 2014 European Championships for removing his shirt in a football-style victory celebration as he came down the finishing straight comfortably clear of his rivals. In a remarkable turnaround, he went back to the Zurich track three days later to win gold in the 1500m. After that race, he paid tribute to the three people who had supported him

---

34. Ibid., p. 97.

35. Anthony Hernandez (with Pierre-Jean Vazel), 'Marie-José Pérec: "Gagner était une question de vie ou de mort"', *Le Monde*, 19 February 2015.

following his disqualification: his coach, Philippe Dupont; his old sparring partner, Mehdi Baala; and the national technical director, Ghani Yalouz.[36] Born in Casablanca, Yalouz won a silver medal in wrestling at the 1996 Olympics and, despite being a non-specialist, was appointed to his current post in 2009, leading the French athletics team to record European medal hauls in Barcelona in 2010 and in Zurich in 2014. Yalouz has characterized his determinedly hands-on approach to competitor-management as 'la méthode palabre', which we might characterize as a sport-specific talking cure which would appear to be paying particular dividends in elite competition.[37] Questioned about Mekhissi-Benabbad's actions, Yalouz responded: 'Le sport, ce n'est jamais lisse. [...] On ne peut jamais prévoir. Il y a ce grain de folie de certains athlètes qui leur a coûté cher mais qui va leur permettre de comprendre que rien n'est acquis.'[38] For his own part, Mekhissi-Benabbad has forcefully asserted the linkage between his migrant heritage, his athletic achievement and his media representation:

> Encore aujourd'hui, on me demande qui je suis, d'où je viens. Je réponds que je suis français. Ça pose un problème à quelqu'un? Je suis français! [...] Nous, enfants d'immigrés, devons faire plus que les autres. On ne démarre pas sur la même ligne: on part en retard, de beaucoup plus loin. On a trop d'obstacles, on doit être meilleur que les autres. Petit, mon père me disait: « *Il n'y a que les meilleurs qui réussissent dans la vie, il n'y a pas de place pour les faibles, il faut être le numéro un.* » J'ai grandi dans un quartier HLM de Reims, la mentalité dans une cité est très simple: c'est l'envie de gagner.[39]

These comments are noteworthy for the runner's strong identification with France, and thus with the national collectivity, in the first half of the quotation, before he moves on to place the emphasis squarely on the uncompromising individualism required of the elite athlete. The complex, and even conflicted, mindset which this reveals may offer a somewhat less attractive image of postcolonial sporting success than the ostensibly harmonious multiculturalism of France's *black-blanc-beur* footballers in 1998, but it may also be a more accurate reflection of the global competitor's lived experience.

Conclusion
By way of a conclusion, we might briefly compare the post-1985 evolution of French football and athletics with that of rugby union. France's first modern team

---

36. Yann Bouchez, 'La belle moisson des athlètes français en Suisse', *Le Monde*, 18 August 2014.
37. Annabelle Rolnin, 'La méthode Yalouz', *L'Équipe*, 3 August 2010.
38. Bouchez, 'La belle moisson'.
39. Mustapha Kessous, 'Mahiedine Mekhissi: "Mon dopage, c'est la foi"', *Le Monde*, 13 July 2012.

game, the fifteen-a-side code was imported from English public (i.e. private) schools in the wake of the Franco-Prussian war, its widespread implantation significantly preceding that of association football. Despite the French game's entrenched ethos of covert payments to players throughout most of the twentieth century, the sport worldwide was officially amateur until 1995, when rugby union belatedly embraced professionalism, thereby prompting not only an institutional upheaval in this most traditional of athletic pursuits, but also a revolution in the mind-sets of players, administrators and supporters. The reconfiguration coincided with that year's Rugby World Cup in newly post-apartheid South Africa and was driven by media corporations originating in the sport's other southern strongholds of Australia and New Zealand. The resistance to change of traditionalist forces in the national rugby federations of Great Britain and Ireland, together with France, was rapidly overwhelmed by new commercial actors and new competitive imperatives. Two decades on from this radical transformation, the French rugby landscape has been transformed, as a variety of often iconoclastic entrepreneurs have used capital derived from successful media operations to revitalize and even resurrect historic clubs. In a passionate rugby enclave far from the game's south-western heartland, the Toulon club has been reimagined by local businessman Mourad Boudjellal, who made his money as a publisher of *bandes dessinées* under the Soleil Productions imprint, including particularly the immigration-themed and often autobiographical work of his elder brother Farid.[40] Recruiting star players from around the rugby world, Boudjellal's Toulon won back-to-back European Champions Cups in 2012–13 and 2013–14, thus making its mark on the now global game.

Important changes have also taken place since 1995 in the composition of the French national side. The make-up of today's professionalized *XV de France* increasingly reflects both the postcolonial diversity of the general population and the new mobility of elite players from the southern hemisphere.[41] The starting team in the first round of the 2015 Six Nations was consequently more newsworthy for its inclusion of three South Africans based in France rather than the tournament debut of a single 'North African'. Following Rabah Slimani's introduction against Scotland, similar starts were given in subsequent rounds to Eddy Ben Arous and the Algiers-born winger Sofiane Guitoune, from the Bordeaux Bègles club. The two prop forwards, Slimani and Ben Arous, come respectively from Trappes (Yvelines) and Sarcelles (Val d'Oise), where they played for their local sides before being discovered by the powerful Racing Métro

---

40. Cathal Kilcline, 'Representations of Rugby and Resistance in Toulon: From Literary Tradition to Televised Spectacle', *Contemporary French Civilization*, 39:1 (2014), 93–110.

41. < http://www.rbs6nations.com/en/france/france_squad.php > [accessed 27 February 2015].

and Stade Français clubs. These Parisian suburbs were the scenes of rioting in 2013 and 2014. However, while the integrative potential of rugby in the *banlieue* has been the subject of recent media attention,[42] coverage of the sporting ascension of Ben Arous and Slimani has remained essentially technical. This may be suggestive of a broader change in attitudes, contrasting notably with the reporting in 1997 of the appointment as French captain of Abdelatif Benazzi, who remains world rugby's most celebrated player of Maghrebian origin, and it is with his case that we shall bring the discussion to a close.

Benazzi was born in Morocco and initially played there, including representing his country as a junior international, before being recruited by the Cahors club, then moving to senior side Agen, going on to play 78 times for France between 1990 and 2001. In his first season in charge of the team, he led the *XV de France* to a Grand Slam of victories over the other competing nations, its first such achievement in a decade. Occurring a full year before the triumph of the country's *black-blanc-beur* football players, this was noteworthy in itself. Moreover, the choice of a North African – additionally, and publicly, a committed Muslim – to lead the national team was by no means only of interest to French rugby watchers given the widespread *Lepénisation des esprits* associated with the period.[43] Benazzi's symbolic stature was underscored later that same year, when he was appointed to the Haut Conseil à l'Intégration by the ever media-aware Jacques Chirac. His combined athletic accomplishments and community credentials would see him hailed in 2000 not only as 'un sportif d'exception', but also as 'un modèle' and, more specifically, 'un grand frère', by the Minister for Employment and Solidarity, Martine Aubry. As the foregoing discussion of football and athletics will have made clear, idealistic declarations of sport's potential for social transformation must be treated with caution, particularly when made by politicians. Nevertheless, Aubry's description of the player and his distinguished contribution to the sporting life of his adopted nation remains worthy of note:

> Un modèle, car son parcours exemplaire (du club marocain d'Oujda au capitanat de l'équipe de France) illustre parfaitement le sens qu'il convient de donner au mot « intégration ». Abdelatif Benazzi a su trouver une place – et quelle place – dans notre société tout en préservant son identité, son attachement à sa culture et à sa religion. Sa réussite est la démonstration éclatante que l'intégration n'est pas l'assimilation par la négation mais bien l'adhésion à un socle de valeurs et de principes communs dans le respect de l'identité et des différences de chacun. C'est ce message, fort, qu'il délivre à tous les jeunes dont les parents viennent d'ailleurs.[44]

---

42. Bruno Lesprit, 'Mêlée sociale à Massy', *Le Monde*, 23 January 2015.

43. Ian Borthwick, 'A Nation Places its Faith in Benazzi', *The Independent*, 1 March 1997.

44. Abdelatif Benazzi (with Jean-Charles Delesalle), *Abdelatif Benazzi: la foi du rugby* (Paris: Solar, 2000), p. 6.

Whatever our reservations about the concept of *intégration* itself, Benazzi's outstanding achievement in a rugby world struggling to come to terms with the shock of the new, combined with his wider record of public service, would seem to argue for cautious optimism as regards the professionally reconfigured game's capacity to encourage diversity in its playing ranks, as in French sport and society more broadly.

Nottingham French Studies 54.3 (2015): 269–282
DOI: 10.3366/nfs.2015.0126
© University of Nottingham
www.euppublishing.com/journal/nfs

LA FRANCE À L'HEURE DE LA MONDIALISATION

CATHERINE WIHTOL DE WENDEN

Un monde en mouvement

Les migrations internationales ont triplé en quarante ans, atteignant aujourd'hui 232 millions de migrants internationaux selon le département de la Population des Nations Unies. Mais, même si le monde bouge, l'essentiel de la population mondiale demeure sédentaire, avec 3,1% seulement de la planète en situation migratoire. Ces migrations, tout en se mondialisant (peu de pays sont aujourd'hui à l'écart des dynamiques de départ, d'arrivée et de transit), se sont aussi fortement régionalisées. Des systèmes migratoires régionaux se dessinent, amorçant des complémentarités entre l'offre et la demande de main d'œuvre autour d'espaces circonscrits par des réseaux linguistiques et culturels transnationaux: le continent nord- américain, l'Amérique du sud, l'Europe et la rive sud de la méditerranée, la Russie et ses voisins, la Turquie et ses voisins, l'Asie du sud-est, le Japon et l'Australie. Beaucoup des migrants se dirigeant vers ces régions sont aussi originaires de ces mêmes régions: Mexicains aux États-Unis, Andins dans le cône sud-américain, Maghrébins et Turcs en Europe, migrants d'Asie centrale en Russie, populations du sud-est asiatique au Japon, en Australie et en Corée du sud[1].

Les catégories de migrants sont devenues de plus en plus floues: à la différence du passé où nombre de réfugiés se distinguaient des travailleurs non qualifiés, aujourd'hui ce sont les mêmes qui tantôt utilisent la demande d'asile, l'accès au marché du travail ou le regroupement familial pour entrer légalement. Des sans-papiers peuvent aussi, au cours de leur vie, emprunter de nombreux statuts s'ils réussissent à se maintenir durablement sur le territoire d'accueil et s'ils sont qualifiés. Enfin, les catégories de pays elles-mêmes sont évolutives car beaucoup de pays de départ sont aussi devenus des pays d'accueil et de transit, comme le Maroc, la Turquie, ou le Mexique. De nouveaux profils de migrants sont apparus également, comme les étudiants qui entrent sur le marché du travail dans le pays de leurs études, les migrants pendulaires qui vivent sur deux espaces connectés entre eux, les déplacés environnementaux, les gardiennes des personnes âgées, les seniors qui s'installent au soleil, les travailleurs à distance du e-business, les

---

1. Catherine Wihtol de Wenden, *Les Nouvelles Migrations* (Paris: Ellipses, 2013).

experts très qualifiés, les femmes, qui constituent aujourd'hui 51% des migrants internationaux...

Mais le changement le plus important est peut-être la nouvelle direction prise par les migrations, avec l'émergence du sud comme destination finale: des pays émergents comme le Brésil, l'Inde, la Chine et l'Afrique du Sud, et, au nord, la Russie, des pays pétroliers comme les pays du Golfe ou l'Angola mais aussi détenteurs de ressources minières comme la Guinée. Environ 130 millions de migrants vont du sud au nord et du nord au nord, mais près de 110 millions vont du sud au sud et du nord au sud: le sud est donc en train de devenir une destination presque aussi importante que le nord en termes de migrations. De multiples transformations en découlent. L'Europe, devenue durant ces trente dernières années, la plus grande région migratoire du monde en termes de flux, est reliée au sud par un ensemble de réseaux sans lesquels il n'y aurait pas de migrations: la communication audiovisuelle, internet et téléphonique, la proximité linguistique, l'existence de liens familiaux déjà constitués avec des migrations antérieures, le voisinage géographique sont de puissants liens migratoires sans compter le passé colonial ou d'anciennes pratiques politiques d'accords bilatéraux de main d'œuvre (Turcs en Allemagne, Marocains en Espagne, Albanais et Tunisiens en Italie, Ukrainiens au Portugal). Des pays de la rive sud de la méditerranée sont devenus, malgré eux, des sas, du fait de la pression exercée par les Européens pour qu'ils ferment leurs frontières à leurs voisins du sud, tout en accueillant à bras ouverts les touristes, les entrepreneurs, leurs diasporas qualifiées et les candidats du nord à l'installation au soleil pour la retraite.

Autre transformation: les pays de destination des réfugiés. Même si l'Europe, les États-Unis, le Canada ont été et continuent d'être de grands pays d'accueil de demandeurs d'asile (qui accèdent d'ailleurs de plus en plus difficilement au statut de réfugié), ce sont l'Iran, le Pakistan, la Turquie, la Syrie, la Jordanie, le Liban qui ont accueilli ces vingt dernières années les victimes des crises du Proche et du Moyen Orient. Les révolutions arabes ont, pour l'essentiel, produit des déplacés chez leurs voisins: Libyens en Tunisie, Tunisiens en Italie et en France, Syriens en Turquie. Le continent africain, grand producteur de réfugiés, est aussi une grande zone d'accueil des déplacés forcés, internationaux et internes. Quant aux déplacés environnementaux, cantonnés pour l'essentiel au sud de la planète, il s'agit pour l'instant essentiellement de migrations du sud au sud et de migrations internes. Leur nombre, d'après les experts, pourrait cependant avoisiner celui des migrants internationaux d'aujourd'hui (soit environ 200 millions) d'ici la fin du siècle.

Ces mutations caractérisent ce qui est souvent considéré comme une seconde grande vague d'immigration de masse, survenue depuis les années 1990, la première se situant entre 1860 et 1930. Mais, bien que les migrations se soient imposées comme une donnée nouvelle, beaucoup de pays refusent cette réalité, notamment en Europe où l'immigration d'installation fait figure de présence illégitime car les pays européens ne se reconnaissent pas comme pays d'immigration de peuplement, bien que ce soit l'immigration qui a permis à la population européenne de croître et de conserver son rang dans la population mondiale, tout en rendant les Européens de l'Union sensiblement plus mobiles que par le passé.

La France

La France affiche une bonne santé démographique comparée à beaucoup de ses voisins européens car elle a cherché plus tôt qu'eux à lutter contre le vieillissement démographique, ayant commencé plus tôt à réduire le nombre de ses naissances. Mais elle doit en partie à l'immigration la croissance de sa population. Comme ailleurs en Europe, le comportement des familles immigrées se conforme progressivement à la taille des familles européennes, avec un nombre d'enfants légèrement supérieur à celui des familles françaises (2,5 enfants par femme contre 2,1). Autre caractéristique: l'inégale répartition de la population sur le territoire et la faible densité de population par rapport à d'autres pays européens. On manque de médecins de campagne, les plus âgés étant remplacés par des médecins roumains et bulgares, qui acceptent de s'installer en milieu rural à la demande des communes. À la campagne, on rencontre aussi une population d'Européens à la recherche d'espace et de maisons anciennes à restaurer. Les Anglais sont les plus nombreux à s'installer à l'année dans l'ouest et le sud-ouest de la France. C'est le « Britishland », qui respecte peu ou prou les anciennes frontières de l'empire des Plantagenêt. Mais on trouve aussi des Néerlandais, des Allemands, seniors au soleil ou actifs d'âge mûr venant créer de nouveaux emplois à distance ou appropriés à leur implantation rurale (bâtiment, restaurants, brocante...)[2].

Après avoir longtemps été le second pays dans l'Union européenne pour le nombre de ses étrangers, après l'Allemagne, la France est devenue, depuis ces cinq dernières années, du fait de sa présence étrangère stable, le cinquième pays d'immigration en Europe, après l'Allemagne, l'Espagne, l'Italie et le Royaume Uni. Ses nationalités les plus nombreuses sont toujours les mêmes qu'il y a trente ans: Portugais, Algériens, Marocains, dans le même ordre d'importance décroissante, suivis ensuite par les Turcs et les Tunisiens. En revanche, si les Anglais, Allemands, commencent à s'imposer dans le paysage migratoire, on constate un recul des Italiens et des Espagnols car leur immigration est ancienne et s'est estompée du fait des acquisitions de nationalité française. L'Afrique sub-saharienne est plus présente qu'il y a trente ans, notamment s'agissant du Mali, du Sénégal et du Congo et de nouvelles nationalités ont fait surface comme les

---

2. Catherine Wihtol de Wenden, *Atlas des migrations: un équilibre mondial à inventer*, troisième édition (Paris: Autrement, 2012).

Pakistanais, Afghans et autres originaires du Proche et du Moyen Orient du fait des crises qui ont sévi dans la région depuis ces trente dernières années. Leur nombre est souvent mal connu en raison de la part des sans-papiers et des demandeurs d'asile selon les nationalités. En revanche, l'impact de la chute du mur de Berlin et de l'ouverture des frontières à l'est est resté faible sur la présence de migrants d'Europe centrale et orientale en France à la différence de l'Allemagne, du Royaume Uni, de l'Irlande, de l'Italie et de la Grèce, en dehors des Roms. Il en va de même des révolutions arabes de 2011: elles ne se sont pas soldées par le déferlement annoncé par certains mais l'instabilité de certains pays du sud de la méditerranée comme la Libye les rend plus vulnérables aux passages clandestins vers l'Europe du sud (Italie notamment).

Si les régions de provenance se sont diversifiées depuis trente ans du fait des crises politiques survenues dans le monde ayant affecté la France par l'arrivée de demandeurs d'asile (Algérie des années 1995, Irak depuis la guerre du Golfe, Afghanistan et crise des grand lacs en Afrique de la fin de la décennie 1990, Syrie aujourd'hui), les populations en présence ne constituent pas de nombres suffisants pour constituer des groupes d'influence de nature à transformer la physionomie de la présence étrangère. Certes, il existe aujourd'hui à Paris une « Little India », qui était moins visible au milieu des années 1980, la succession des nationalités s'est poursuivie dans l'ancien quartier algérien de la Goutte d'or devenu chinois et africain, la présence turque s'est amplifiée dans le quartier de Strasbourg Saint-Denis, le quartier asiatique de la Porte de Choisy des années 1975 a vieilli, les générations suivantes ayant tendance à se fondre dans la population française. Mais le poids démographique des étrangers ne compte pas pour une plus grande part de la population française qu'il y a trente ans, compte tenu du fait que le nombre des descendants de l'immigration devenus Français ne figure pas parmi les statistiques des étrangers. La plupart des ressortissants hors Union européenne admis au séjour permanent sont, d'après le rapport SOPEMI de l'OCDE, originaires d'Afrique (pour 60%), particulièrement d'Afrique du Nord (30%). L'Asie est la deuxième région de provenance (20%), suivie par les pays d'Europe hors de l'Union européenne. Le nombre de demandes d'asile, qui a dépassé 50 000 par an depuis ces trois dernières années, fait de la France, tour à tour avec la Suède, l'Allemagne et le Royaume Uni, le premier ou le second pays d'accueil en Europe[3].

Cent-cinquante ans d'immigration et de politiques migratoires
L'immigration a commencé à se développer dans la seconde moitié du dix-neuvième siècle, du fait du déclin démographique de la France, amorcé dès la fin du dix-huitième siècle, dans un contexte de révolution industrielle

---

3.   OCDE, SOPEMI (Paris), *Perspectives des migrations internationales,* rapports annuels.

nécessitant une abondante main d'œuvre. Les pays voisins constituaient des réservoirs de main d'œuvre (Belges, Italiens, Allemands, Suisses dès les années 1880, puis Polonais), ainsi que l'immigration coloniale avant et surtout après la fin de la première guerre mondiale (Algériens de Kabylie et des Aurès). Terre d'accueil, au lendemain de la première guerre mondiale, pour les victimes de l'effondrement des grands empires (Turquie, Russie, Autriche Hongrie), la France leur donne le statut de réfugiés (en utilisant notamment le passeport Nansen pour les Russes et les Arméniens rendus apatrides par leur pays d'origine). En 1932, la France comptait déjà 3 millions d'étrangers et était le premier pays d'immigration d'Europe, les Italiens étant les plus nombreux. Puis viennent des vagues successives de réfugiés: Espagnols avec la guerre civile et autres fugitifs du fascisme (*fuorisciti*) et du nazisme.

La fin de la seconde guerre mondiale ouvre une nouvelle donne, avec l'entrée dans les « trente glorieuses » (1945–1974), qui introduit une période de croissance économique exceptionnelle dans un contexte persistant de manque de main d'œuvre. Dès lors, ce sont les pouvoirs publics (et non plus le patronat, comme durant l'entre-deux guerres avec la Société générale d'Immigration) qui gèrent l'immigration. L'ordonnance de 1945 sur l'entrée et le séjour des étrangers (toujours en vigueur) et la loi de 1945 sur le droit de la nationalité dessinent un cadre pour la politique migratoire. Mais très vite, la distinction, doublée par une politique nataliste définie par le démographe Alfred Sauvy, entre l'immigration de travail et l'immigration de peuplement, est dépassée par les besoins de main d'oeuvre (reconstruction, politique de logement, industries automobiles, sidérurgie, mines, agriculture). Les Italiens, décriés dans les années 1930, apparaissent comme une immigration désirable mais ils viennent moins nombreux que prévu à cause du « miracle économique » des années 1960. Une succession de vagues migratoires est introduite par le patronat souvent clandestinement: Espagnols, Portugais (dont la France est toujours le premier pays d'accueil), Algériens, Yougoslaves, Turcs, Marocains, Tunisiens et Africains sub-sahariens (Mali, Mauritanie, Sénégal).

Le paysage migratoire se transforme: pour la première fois au recensement de 1975, les non-Européens sont plus nombreux que les Européens parmi les immigrés. Dans le même temps, l'immigration de main d'œuvre rurale et souvent analphabète qui faisait des allers retours au pays, commence à se sédentariser du fait de la suspension de l'immigration de travail salarié en juillet 1974. Le nouveau président de la République, Valéry Giscard d'Estaing vient de nommer (pour la première fois depuis le Front Populaire) un secrétaire d'Etat à l'immigration, André Postel Vinay, qui démissionne au bout de deux mois faute de moyens pour une politique du logement. Son successeur, Paul Dijoud, jette les bases d'une politique d'intégration. Les immigrés vivent dans les bidonvilles qui entourent les grandes métropoles (Paris, Lyon, Marseille, Nice) et dans les foyers pour isolés qui sont eux aussi parfois insalubres. Une politique de résorption des bidonvilles a été entamée par Jacques Chaban-Delmas en 1969. Mais la suspension de l'immigration de travail bloque la mobilité et le regroupement familial s'accélère, faisant émerger la question des « secondes générations » et de l'intégration, dans les banlieues lyonnaises, puis parisiennes, sur fond d'émergence de l'islam, deuxième religion de France. Alors que les nouveaux Européens de pays entrés dans l'Union européenne passent de la clandestinité à la légalité, comme les Portugais, les non Européens sont assujettis à visas (dont les Algériens qui avaient jusque-là bénéficié de la libre circulation aux termes des accords d'Evian). La question des sans-papiers marque la fin du septennat de Valéry Giscard d'Estaing, à l'aube des années 1980. C'est alors qu'une frénésie législative s'empare de la politique migratoire, qui n'avait été l'objet d'aucune loi entre 1945 et 1980.

A partir de 1981, chaque alternance gouvernementale se traduit par une nouvelle loi sur l'immigration et l'on en compte plus de 25 depuis cette date. La période 1981–1984 marque la régularisation de 142 000 sans-papiers, la liberté d'association pour les étrangers (1981), une législation sur l'entrée et le séjour plus respectueuse des droits, avec notamment l'adoption de la carte de résidence de dix ans, en 1984, suite à la marche des beurs de 1983. Les immigrés installés de longue date peuvent résider automatiquement en France quelle que soit leur situation de travail. Cette décision marque la consolidation de l'immigration familiale. Mais la montée du Front national, aux municipales de 1983 change la donne. Peu à peu l'immigration devient un thème sécuritaire et fortement politisé[4]. Parallèlement, la politique européenne s'inscrit dans la politique nationale. Après l'adoption des accords de Schengen en 1985, et l'acquis communautaire (ensemble des dispositifs européens de contrôle des frontières), c'est en 1993, avec la loi Pasqua que, pour la première fois, le dispositif européen devient partie intégrante de la législation française. La dimension sécuritaire, dissuasive et répressive s'amplifie et les droits des étrangers sont précarisés. L'exemple le plus significatif est le droit d'asile: alors que dans les années 1970, près de 80% des demandeurs d'asile recevaient le statut de réfugié de la Convention de Genève, dans les années 1990 ils ne sont plus que 20% à obtenir de ce statut, alors que les conflits et crises politiques mettent sur les routes de l'Europe des milliers de réfugiés. La question des sans-papiers devient cruciale, tandis que la politique affichée est celle de l' « immigration zéro » et que le droit du sol dans l'accès à la nationalité est restreint (loi Pasqua-Méhaignerie de 1993).

---

4.   Catherine Wihtol de Wenden, *Les Immigrés et la politique: cent-cinquante ans d'évolution* (Paris: Presses de la FNSP, 1988). Voir aussi Patrick Weil, *La France et ses étrangers* (Paris: Calmann-Lévy, 1995) et, du même auteur, *Qu'est-ce qu'un français? Histoire de la nationalité française depuis la révolution* (Paris: Gallimard, 2004) ainsi que *Histoire de l'immigration et des étrangers en France*, dir. par Yves Lequin (Paris: Larousse, 2006).

En 1997, une nouvelle régularisation légalise 90 000 sans-papiers et la loi Guigou de 1998 revient à l'équilibre droit du sol/droit du sang dans l'accès à la nationalité.

Plusieurs rapports internationaux commencent alors à questionner le bien-fondé de la fermeture des frontières. En 2000, un rapport du département de la Population des Nations Unies sur les migrations de remplacement dresse le scenario des besoins d'immigration pour répondre aux besoins de main d'œuvre, rétablir, en Europe (comme en Russie et au Japon), le ratio entre les actifs et les inactifs et l'équilibre de la pyramide des âges. Un Livre vert européen de 2005 prône l'entrouverture des frontières aux très qualifiés, la réponse aux besoins de main d'œuvre et à l'immigration nécessaire pour rester dans la compétitivité internationale. Plusieurs pays européens, comme l'Allemagne et le Royaume Uni adoptent des politiques sélectives de l'immigration avec des permis à points inspirés du Canada, tandis que la France adopte la loi Sarkozy de 2006 sur l'immigration choisie (pour les « capacités et talents », avec des séjours saisonniers pour les métiers manuels et des listes de « métiers en tension », qualifiés et non qualifiés).

Mais la politique d'immigration se durcit progressivement, dans un contexte de montée de l'extrême droite: objectifs chiffrés de reconductions à la frontière (entre 25 000 et 35 000 par an pendant la période 2007–2012), accent mis (y compris dans l'intitulé du Ministère de l'Immigration, de l'Intégration, de l'Identité nationale et du Développement Solidaire) sur l'identité nationale (2007), débat sur les retraits de nationalité française (une pratique effectuée sous le gouvernement de Vichy pour les juifs naturalisés), accélération des accords bilatéraux de reconductions à la frontière avec les pays de la rive sud de la méditerranée (avec 15 accords, dont la Libye a été l'un des interlocuteurs les plus zélés, avec la Tunisie), fermeture médiatisée de la « jungle » de Sangatte où campaient notamment les Afghans, en attente de passer au Royaume-Uni (2009), conclusion en 2008 du Pacte européen sur l'immigration et l'asile dressant les cinq points d'une politique européenne de l'immigration, mais sans valeur contraignante (introduire l'immigration nécessaire aux besoins du marché du travail dans les limites des capacités d'intégration, renforcer le contrôle des frontières, lutter contre l'immigration clandestine, harmoniser le droit d'asile, conclure des accords bi ou multilatéraux avec les pays d'origine pour renvoyer les sans-papiers en échange de politiques de développement et de titres de séjour pour les plus qualifiés). En 2011, la politique d'immigration cherche à restreindre le regroupement familial, refuse l'accès au marché du travail aux étudiants et ferme la frontière franco-italienne de Vintimille après l'arrivée à Lampedusa de quelques 28 000 Tunisiens suite aux révolutions arabes. L'année suivante Nicolas Sarkozy fait du thème de l'étranger un instrument-clé dans sa campagne présidentielle, notamment dans le discours qu'il prononce à Villepinte en mars 2012.

La politique qui a suivi la victoire de la gauche en 2012 a introduit quelques modifications comme notamment le titre de séjour pluriannuel, l'abolition de la circulaire de 2011 interdisant aux étudiants l'accès au marché du travail, sans changer le mélange d'entrouverture (liste des métiers en tension rétablie en 2008, mais avec 30 métiers au lieu de 14) et de contrôle suivie précédemment, mais elle a cessé de faire de la politique d'immigration un outil de séduction de l'électorat d'extrême droite. Le droit de vote local des étrangers, 50ème proposition du candidat Hollande n'a toujours pas été mis à l'agenda. Avec 163 000 entrées en 2012[5], la France enregistre une augmentation de la demande d'asile (66 000 en 2013 et 64 800 en 2014) et du nombre de regroupements familiaux, avec un recul de l'immigration de travail et d'étudiants. Les nouveaux arrivants admis au séjour permanent sont, en flux annuels, en majorité des Maghrébins (Algériens, Marocains, Tunisiens), suivis par les Chinois et les Turcs, puis les Sénégalais, Maliens et Camerounais. La France est le second pays dans le monde pour l'accueil de demandeurs d'asile au titre de la convention de Genève, derrière les États-Unis et le premier en Europe. Les 160 000 acquisitions de nationalité franç aise (par décret, par mariage et anticipations de mineurs) dont 96 000 naturalisations, expliquent, depuis plusieurs années, un nombre d'étrangers resté stable, le nombre des étrangers entrant sur le territoire national avoisinant celui des personnes précédemment étrangères devenus nouveaux Français. En stocks, les Portugais restent les plus nombreux (près de 500 000) depuis le recensement de 1982, suivis par les Algériens (470 000), les Marocains (450 000) et les Turcs (240 000).

Quarante ans de politiques d'accueil
Face à ces flux migratoires, la question de l'intégration par les politiques urbaines, le dialogue avec l'Islam dans l'espace public, la lutte contre les discriminations et la définition du vivre ensemble ne cesse de susciter pendant toute cette période d'importants débats. C'est en 1974 que, suite à la suspension de l'immigration de travail salarié en France, une politique d'accueil est lancée par Paul Dijoud avec le concours d'un réseau associatif, qui devient réseau national d'accueil des immigrés. Ce réseau d'accueil était lui-même très diversifié, nourri de mouvances variées et d'actions ciblées auprès de populations d'origines multiples. Il pouvait paraître contradictoire de développer une politique d'accueil au moment où l'on suspendait l'arrivée de l'immigration de travail. Celle-ci était surtout arrivée dans le désordre, par suite du manque de main d'œuvre dans une période de croissance économique qui s'achevait en 1974 après les « Trente Glorieuses ». L'accueil de la période précédente concernait les primo-arrivants, parfois analphabètes, logés dans des foyers ou des bidonvilles, arrimés au monde du travail. La politique d'accueil de Paul Dijoud et de ses successeurs va alors se déployer autour d'autres

---

5.   OCDE, *Perspectives des migrations internationales 2014* (Paris: OECD, 2014), p. 359.

populations – les familles, les générations issues de l'immigration, les réfugiés – tout en conservant son ancrage auprès des primo-migrants déjà installés, dans l'aide aux papiers, au logement, à l'alphabétisation.

Où en est-on aujourd'hui, quarante ans après? La politique d'accueil, longtemps financée par le FAS (Fonds d'Action Sociale), devenu FASILD au tournant des années 2000 pour signifier son engagement dans la lutte contre les discriminations, puis ACSE et enfin fondue dans une structure plus large, L'Office français de l'immigration et de l'intégration, a souvent souffert des contradictions de la politique d'immigration et de ses revirements, au gré des alternances politiques. Respect du droit en 1981, période associative civique entre 1983 (marche des beurs) et 1993 (lois Pasqua), chute des financements publics au milieu des années 1990 et ancrage européen, lutte contre les discriminations des années 2000, accent mis sur la citoyenneté, la laïcité et l'identité française dans les années 2003–2012 – autant de points ponctuant l'évolution à laquelle on assiste pendant cette période.

L'une des difficultés de la politique d'accueil a été à la fois de contribuer à la mise en œuvre de la politique publique d'intégration à la française et de conserver un esprit militant en faveur du respect des droits des étrangers. Car comment peut-on accueillir d'un côté si l'on mène une politique restrictive à l'entrée et au séjour de l'autre qui nuit à l'intégration future des nouveaux entrants? Tel a été le dilemme, car beaucoup de décideurs politiques ont considéré que les clandestins nuisaient à l'intégration de ceux qui sont là.

A Lyon, l'importance des bidonvilles démolis ensuite au profit des cités de grands ensembles a vu naître une mouvance associative de solidarité avec les immigrés mais aussi, dès la fin des 1970, les premières émeutes urbaines des jeunes dits de « seconde génération », point de départ de la marche des « beurs », pour l'égalité et contre le racisme de 1983. En 1981, la loi qui accorde la liberté d'association aux étrangers sur le modèle de la loi de 1901 favorise en effet la création d'associations civiques issues de l'immigration qui travaillent parallèlement à l'accueil avec les associations de première génération, caritatives ou de solidarité militante (mais souvent sans lien avec elles). Outre le mouvement « beur » qui en est issu, ce sera le début, au tournant des années 1990, d'une municipalisation de la vie associative, mise au service de l'action de lutte contre les violences urbaines, d'actions d'intégration auprès des « secondes générations » et de lutte contre les discriminations et pour la promotion de la diversité culturelle. L'accueil des primo arrivants persiste, mais il se concentre sur d'autres populations qu'à l'époque des travailleurs étrangers: femmes, (alors que les précédents étaient majoritairement des hommes), demandeurs d'asile, mineurs non accompagnés, ces deux dernières catégories étant fortement représentées dans la région Rhône Alpes.

A partir de 1993, la politique d'immigration se durcit, les subventions aux associations diminuent et l'inhospitalité fait parfois figure de mode de fonctionnement de l'accueil à travers les politiques de « guichet ». L'esprit de dissuasion orchestré à l'échelon européen se répercute sur la précarisation du statut des étrangers en France, sous la pression de la montée du Front national: sans-papiers, déboutés du droit d'asile. De nouveaux profils se font jour au tournant des années 2000, des immigrés âgés (souvent des hommes seuls marqués par le monde du travail), des familles monoparentales, des femmes venues seules, de jeunes primo arrivants, des mineurs non accompagnés. Bien souvent, les conditions d'entrée ont des répercussions sur la poursuite du séjour en France, car quelle politique d'accueil peut-on envisager pour ceux qui sont longtemps maintenus dans la précarité du séjour?

L'accueil s'enracine dans l'insertion linguistique et culturelle des nouveaux entrants, avec le contrat d'accueil et d'intégration exigé pour les immigrés entrés légalement en France. Il se déploie dans la vie associative des cités à travers la thématique de la diversité culturelle, dans la lutte contre les discriminations, dans le soutien scolaire, perdant un peu au passage le militantisme associatif des premiers jours ou au contraire mobilisant des militants d'une cause: l'ouverture des frontières. Nombre d'associations nationales mais aussi avec leurs antennes régionales et locales, comme RESF (Réseau Éducation sans frontières), la Ligue des droits de l'Homme, la FASTI (Fédération de solidarité avec les travailleurs immigrés), le MRAP (Mouvement contre le racisme et pour l'amitié entre les peuples), le Secours catholique, la CIMADE-Service œcuménique d'entraide, l'ACAT (Association des chrétiens contre la torture) et quelques autres ont su fédérer autour d'elles des militants du quotidien qui s'occupent d'une autre forme d'accueil: celui des sans-papiers, des déboutés du droit d'asile, des individus isolés et des familles en instance de reconduction à la frontière en les aidant à constituer leurs dossiers de régularisation et parfois aussi en leur apportant des soins de première nécessité (couvertures, nourriture, abri). Elles agissent souvent dans l'urgence, dans l'affrontement avec les pouvoirs publics, dans le plaidoyer national et parfois international (Forums sociaux mondiaux). De leur côté, Forum Réfugiés et France Terre d'Asile se spécialisent dans l'accueil des demandeurs d'asile. Un autre dilemme de l'accueil se profile: faut-il faire avec ou lutter contre les pouvoirs publics? Beaucoup d'associations sont partagées par l'une et l'autre fonction, collaborative et tribunicienne.

Globalement, la politique d'accueil à la française a institutionnalisé le mouvement associatif au service de la politique publique d'intégration, dans une logique de « faire faire », de délégation de compétences aux associations à l'échelon local, dans un souci d'efficacité et avec moins de moyens.

Trente ans de débats sur le droit de vote local des étrangers non européens
En France, on en parle depuis trente ans. Ceux qui tentent de ranimer le débat rappellent que déjà, en 1981, ce thème faisait partie des cent-une propositions du candidat socialiste François Mitterrand aux élections présidentielles

et qu'auparavant, Jacques Chirac, dans une allocution aux maires des capitales francophones, en 1977, s'y était déclaré favorable[6]. En 1985, François Mitterrand avait ajouté, dans un discours au congrès de la Ligue des droits de l'Homme, qu'il y était personnellement favorable mais que l'opinion publique n'était pas prête et qu'il fallait l'aider. Par la suite, à chaque élection présidentielle, le droit de vote des étrangers est revenu au centre des débats, Jacques Chirac faisant de son opposition au droit de vote son cheval de bataille aux présidentielles de 1988. Nicolas Sarkozy s'y déclarait favorable jusqu'en 2005 avant de s'y opposer. Par la suite, Ségolène Royal, candidate aux élections présidentielles de 2007 s'est prononcée en sa faveur et François Hollande, candidat en 2012, a fait de cette proposition la cinquantième de son programme présenté sous le signe du changement. Les méandres de la reconnaissance du droit de vote et de l'éligibilité locale des étrangers non communautaires ont emprunté toutes les hésitations du débat politique, partagé entre les sondages, longtemps défavorables, puis à partir de 2011 marquant une majorité d'opinions pour (59%), vite suivie par un retournement, passant successivement de 62% à 56% contre, entre septembre 2012 et février 2013, pour se retrouver à l'équilibre entre les « pour » et les « contre ».

Entretemps, la mise en application du traité de Maastricht de 1992 (en son article 8 qui définit la citoyenneté européenne), a conduit à lever une partie des obstacles juridiques qui s'opposaient à la reconnaissance de la citoyenneté locale des étrangers, par la dissociation qu'il opérait entre la citoyenneté et la nationalité, une dissociation qui existait déjà dans les constitutions révolutionnaires. Avec Maastricht, on pouvait désormais être citoyen européen sans être national, comme du temps de la révolution française où en 1791, des conventionnels étrangers comme l'anglais Thomas Paine et le néerlandais Anarcharsis von Clootz ont été élevés à la qualité de citoyens et dans la Constitution de 1793 des étrangers ont été faits citoyens pour services rendus à la cause publique, ou lors de la Commune de Paris en 1871. La modification de la Constitution française qui a suivi la signature du traité de Maastricht étendait la citoyenneté au niveau local et au Parlement européen aux citoyens de l'Union européenne. Ils acquéraient désormais la possibilité d'être électeurs et éligibles à l'échelon local sans être maires ni pouvoir voter dans le collège relatif à la désignation des sénateurs car il leur restait interdit d'exercer une partie de la souveraineté nationale (article 3 de la Constitution). Le débat s'est poursuivi au sein des deux assemblées: tandis qu'à la faveur d'une « niche parlementaire » à l'initiative des Verts à l'Assemblée nationale, le 3 mai 2000, un texte était proposé et voté, le Sénat ne l'a pas mis à l'ordre du jour à l'époque. Passé pour la première fois à gauche depuis la Constitution de 1958, le Sénat a voté le 8 décembre 2011

---

6.   Wihtol de Wenden, *Les Immigrés et la politique*. Voir aussi le dossier « Droit de vote des étrangers: où en est-on ? », *Migrations Société*, 25:146 (printemps 2013).

un texte accordant le droit de vote et l'éligibilité aux étrangers non communautaires, mais en termes légèrement différents de ceux de 2000. On en restait donc au statu quo, le texte devant être voté dans les mêmes termes par les deux assemblées. La non reconnaissance du droit de vote et de l'éligibilité locale a suscité un militantisme associatif soutenu par plusieurs organisations internationales comme le Conseil de l'Europe, le Parlement européen puis l'Union européenne.

Avec l'Europe également, le thème de la citoyenneté de résidence a progressivement servi de fondement au droit de vote, les associations arguant que des étrangers non communautaires installés depuis plus de vingt ans n'étaient pas consultés à la différence des Européens, au séjour de plus courte durée et pourtant citoyens et que dans certaines communes, le nombre des étrangers non communautaires qui y vivent, y travaillent et paient des impôts est si important que la légitimité démocratique des élus est mal assurée. À l'automne 2012, 77 parlementaires, inquiets de voir la cinquantième proposition du programme présidentiel oubliée des priorités gouvernementales, ont lancé une pétition, à l'initiative du député de Seine-Saint Denis Razzi Hammadi. En janvier 2013, le Premier Ministre Jean-Marc Ayrault sort à nouveau le droit de vote des oubliettes et François Hollande, lors de l'inauguration du Musée de l'Immigration à Paris le 15 décembre 2014, a déclaré qu'il incombait aux parlementaires de « prendre leurs responsabilités » sur le droit de vote aux étrangers, mesure à laquelle il restait favorable sans pour autant l'aborder dans ses discours à la nation.

L'année 2013, proclamée année européenne des citoyens, n'a pas permis de relancer le débat sur la citoyenneté européenne de résidence, tout en soulignant les lacunes persistantes: la frontière juridique qui s'est creusée depuis le traité de Maastricht entre étrangers européens et non européens, le fait que l'accès à la citoyenneté européenne soit lié aux règles (différentes) d'acquisition de la nationalité dans chaque pays européen, le développement de nationalités « outre étatiques » du fait de la délivrance de passeports européens à des nationaux vivant hors de leur pays depuis parfois une très longue date, fondée sur des critères ethniques ou historiques (*Aussiedler* en Allemagne depuis 1989, Hongrois d'Ukraine, Italiens d'Amérique latine et d'Australie). Enfin, ce débat ancien, sorte de serpent de mer politique, est mouvant car les arguments pour ou contre ont changé de nature. L'immigré, hier considéré comme un travailleur voué au retour et, tout au plus à l'égalité des droits sociaux et syndicaux, commence à être vu, avec le droit de vote local dans les pays qui l'ont mis en œuvre, comme un futur citoyen, à la différence des pays d'immigration de peuplement comme le nouveau monde (Etats-Unis, Canada, Australie, Nouvelle Zélande) qui ont rapidement accordé l'accès à la nationalité et le droit du sol aux nouveaux venus. Grâce au Traité européen de Maastricht de 1992, la citoyenneté a pu être dissociée de la nationalité, ce qui était impensable aux yeux de nombreux constitutionnalistes voici quarante ans. Enfin, la frilosité manifestée à l'égard de la citoyenneté locale des étrangers s'inscrirait dans la faible volonté en France de mettre en œuvre tous les instruments d'intégration préconisés par l'Europe, ce qu'illustre la publication en février 2013 du rapport Thuot sur les déficits de la politique d'inclusion à la française[7], ou, plus encore, dans la réticence des élus locaux à élargir leur électorat, conduisant à une « démocratie confisquée ».

D'autres débats sont restés sans réponse. Celui lancé, à l'initiative de Nicolas Sarkozy et de ses ministres de l'Immigration, de l'Intégration, de l'identité nationale et du développement solidaire, Brice Hortefeux et Eric Besson sur l'identité nationale s'est soldé par un échec, faute d'adhésion de la société franç aise à un tel débat. La question de l'islam, qui a connu de multiples épisodes avec les affaires du foulard, en 1989, le vote de la loi de 2004 interdisant peu ou prou le port du foulard à l'école, et surtout les attaques terroristes de 1995 (affaire Kelkal), de 2012 (affaire Merah) et de 2015 (affaires Kouachi et Coulibaly), reste sensible et mal résolue dans la tentative de dialogue avec les pouvoirs publics, dans un contexte où le nombre de mosquées a été multiplié par trois depuis trente ans.

Conclusion

« Serons-nous encore Français dans trente ans? » interrogeait, non sans provocation, *Le Figaro magazine* en octobre 1985[8]. En 2015, ces trente ans sont déjà passés et la réponse est toujours affirmative malgré les aléas des débats politiques marqués par la mainmise de l'extrême droite sur le débat identitaire, les malentendus autour de la laïcité « à la française », la diversification des flux migratoires et les atermoiements des politiques du vivre ensemble. Si la France n'a pu « choisir » l'ensemble de ses immigrés, selon le terme d'immigration « choisie » utilisée par Nicolas Sarkozy en 2006 lors du vote de la loi qui porte son nom, la continuité l'emporte de très loin sur le changement. Les raisons en sont multiples: du fait de son ancienneté dans le phénomène migratoire, la France connaît des flux marqués par son passé, puisque l'essentiel des nouvelles entrées provient du regroupement familial. Les autres flux sont liés aux accords internationaux: les réfugiés, fruit des accords de Genève de 1951 sur le droit d'asile, les entrées d'Européens, résultat de la construction européenne qui s'est enrichie de nouveaux bénéficiaires de la liberté de circulation, d'installation et de travail venus depuis 1985 (Grecs et Espagnols en 1986, Portugais en 1992, Finlandais, Autrichiens et Suédois depuis 1995, Maltais et Chypriotes en 2004, Européens de l'Est en 2011, Roumains et Bulgares en 2014), les étudiants, du fait d'une politique d'attraction destinée à assurer le rayonnement français et

---

7. Thierry Tuot, *La Grande Nation: pour une société inclusive*, rapport au Premier Ministre (Paris: La Documentation Française, 2013).

8. 'Dossier immigration: serons-nous encore français dans 30 ans?', *Le Figaro magazine*, 26 octobre 1985.

européen à l'étranger, enfin les migrations de travail, soumises à des restrictions pour les non Européens (préférence européenne à l'emploi) mais aussi à une sélection des compétences et des talents, venus moins nombreux que prévu par la loi sur l' « immigration choisie » de 2006. L'identité française reste marquée par son idéal républicain et laïque, dont le contenu est devenu plus ambigu du fait des courants politiques parfois opposés qui s'en réclament (extrême droite et gauche ultra-laïque) mais elle est évolutive, au gré de la diversité des populations qui négocient avec elle leur place dans la société française.

Nottingham French Studies 54.3 (2015): 283–296
DOI: 10.3366/nfs.2015.0127
© University of Nottingham
www.euppublishing.com/journal/nfs

DÉBATTRE SUR L'IDENTITÉ NATIONALE: L'IMMIGRATION ET L'INTÉGRATION EN QUESTION

YVAN GASTAUT

En novembre 2009, le gouvernement présidé par Nicolas Sarkozy lance en fanfare un vaste débat sur l'identité nationale en France. Innovateur dans sa forme – c'est la première fois qu'un gouvernement français décide de son propre chef d'organiser un débat sur ce sujet en invitant l'ensemble de la population nationale à y participer – ce débat s'insère sur le fond dans une longue série de convulsions qui depuis les années 1980 ne cessent d'agiter la sphère publique. Une thématique revient de manière récurrente dans ces débats: celle d'une « invasion » qui menacerait de détruire la nation française. Des notions de ce genre s'inscrivent dans une continuité qu'il serait aisé de faire remonter à l'Antiquité avec les fameuses « invasions barbares » ou au Moyen-Âge avec la pression des Sarrasins faisant de l'épisode de 732, lorsque Charles Martel repousse les « Arabes » à Poitiers, un point de repère connu aujourd'hui de tous, que les avis hostiles à la présence de migrants maghrébins n'hésitent pas à rappeler. Avec tant de popularité, d'aucuns n'hésitent pas à faire usage de la figure de Jeanne d'Arc pour faire écho à la nécessaire lutte du temps présent contre « l'envahisseur » susceptible de mettre en péril l'identité nationale. Pour la seule période qui commence avec la Troisième République, le spectre d'une arrivée massive de populations pauvres venues d'ailleurs gagne les esprits. Omniprésente à la fin du dix-neuvième siècle et pendant l'entre-deux-guerres pour stigmatiser les Juifs mais aussi les réfugiés russes, arméniens, italiens ou espagnols, cette angoisse collective est révélée par divers écrits parmi lesquels le roman de Louis Bertrand datant de 1907 et intitulé *L'Invasion* décrivant comment l'afflux sans discontinu d'Italiens dans la région marseillaise a marqué son époque[1]. Mêlant réalités et fantasme, le thème de la France envahie par les immigrés devient un discours commode, propagé par de nombreux canaux au premier rang desquels se trouve une extrême droite influente.

Héritier de cette tradition, Jean-Marie Le Pen, qui en 1972 fonde le Front National, en fait un argument électoraliste fécond à partir des années 1980 en martelant à qui veut l'entendre: « On livre le peuple français à une véritable

---

1. Louis Bertrand, *L'Invasion* (Paris: Fasquelle, 1907).

invasion des immigrés »[2]. Mais, au delà du Front national, dans le contexte d'une médiatisation accrue de la « question de l'immigration » au cours des années quatre-vingt, différents milieux politiques s'emparent du terme « invasion » et de son système de représentations, notamment autour de métaphores en lien avec les éléments naturels ou météorologiques. Les propos d'Alain Peyrefitte dans son essai remarqué *Le Mal français* en 1976, en donnent une illustration: « La nature a horreur du vide. Dans un monde sans frontières, la coexistence de hautes et de basses pressions démographiques est génératrice de perturbations. Une osmose violente ce serait une invasion, comme la France en a déjà connu tellement. Une osmose pacifique: ce sera l'invasion déjà commencée d'immigrants »[3].

Il faut dire que ces prises de position sont nourries par des thèses de scientifiques de grand renom prônant la lutte contre la dénatalité et le vieillissement de la population. Celles du démographe Alfred Sauvy (1898–1990) sont les plus connues du grand public, livrant dès les années soixante des analyses scientifiques alarmistes sur l'évolution d'une France condamnée inexorablement à une invasion de populations étrangères venues du Tiers monde. Un essai publié en 1987, au titre emblématique *L'Europe submergée*[4], y fait directement référence dans le sillage de son célèbre ouvrage publié en 1973, *Croissance zéro* dans lequel, en usant des codes de la littérature d'anticipation, Alfred Sauvy décrit une invasion maritime de la France par un bateau venu du Pakistan[5]. Dans un futur proche, une centaine d'affamés Pakistanais ou Bengalis s'embarquent sur un vieux bateau à la recherche d'une terre pour survivre. Après plusieurs mois d'errance, ils échouent sur les côtes du Sud de la France. Alerté, le gouvernement français envoie des gendarmes et des CRS sur les côtes. En dépit des sommations que ces *boat people* ne comprennent pas, les passagers mettent des chaloupes à l'eau, chargées de femmes et d'enfants. Les gendarmes n'osent pas tirer. Pour ne pas compromettre la saison touristique qui bat son plein, les réfugiés sont rapidement envoyés à l'intérieur du pays, et parqués dans un village presqu'abandonné des Alpes de Haute Provence. C'est à ce moment qu'on apprend le départ d'un second bateau du Pakistan…

Inspiré par ce type d'études, le romancier Jean Raspail exploite cette thématique pour son ouvrage *Le Camp des saints,* paru en 1973 et présenté de manière spectaculaire en service de presse: « Dans la nuit sur les côtes du midi de la France, cent navires à bout de souffle se sont échoués, chargés d'un million d'immigrants. Venus du Gange, ils sont l'avant garde du Tiers-monde qui envahit pacifiquement l'Occident pour y trouver l'espérance. À tous les niveaux,

---

2.   Par exemple, *Antenne 2*, émission « L'Heure de Vérité », 14 février 1984.
3.   Alain Peyrefitte, *Le Mal français* (Paris: Fayard, 1976).
4.   Alfred Sauvy, *L'Europe submergée, le Nord et le Sud dans 30 ans* (Paris: Dunod, 1987).
5.   Alfred Sauvy, *Croissance zéro* (Paris: Calmann-Lévy, 1973).

conscience universelle, gouvernement, équilibre des civilisations, et surtout chacun en soi-même, on se pose la question, mais trop tard: que faire? »[6].

C'est ce curieux assemblage mêlant analyse scientifique et récit romancé que *Le Figaro magazine* présente en 1985 sous la houlette de Louis Pauwels et Alain Griotteray dans le dossier « Serons-nous encore français dans trente ans? »[7], qui active le mythe de l'invasion en proposant sur la couverture la photographie d'un buste de Marianne recouvert d'un tchador. Cet ensemble, rédigé sous la plume du démographe Gérard-François Dumont, auquel Alfred Sauvy et Jean Raspail apportent leur concours, explique chiffre à l'appui comment la France de 2015 aura été envahie par les ENE (Étrangers d'origine Non Européenne, c'est-à-dire des populations d'origine immigrée – migrants et leurs descendants – issues pour la plupart de territoires anciennement colonisés).

Cette angoisse qui ne cesse depuis cette période d'alimenter les fantasmes à l'image des propos de Valéry Giscard d'Estaing en 1991 assimilant l'immigration à une invasion[8], s'est renouvelée ces derniers temps avec la théorie du « grand remplacement » porté par quelques écrivains, intellectuels et hommes politiques qui trouve un bel écho dans les médias depuis le début des années 2010[9]. Par exemple, parmi les conséquences des révolutions dans le monde arabe au début de l'année 2011, les mouvements de populations venues du sud de la Méditerranée vers l'Europe est l'une de celles qui retiennent le plus l'attention. Plus particulièrement, l'arrivée en France de plusieurs milliers de Tunisiens et Libyens clandestins transitant par la petite île italienne de Lampedusa depuis le mois de janvier 2011 n'a pas manqué de susciter l'émotion autour du thème de « l'invasion ». Chiffres inquiétants, douaniers s'estimant « submergés », reportages spectaculaires dans les journaux télévisés, opinion excitée au sujet du contrôle des frontières: la crainte d'un afflux massif et continu de Maghrébins dans l'Hexagone a mené le Ministre de l'Intérieur à effectuer une visite « sur le terrain ». Sur fond de tension franco-italienne mettant en évidence les vicissitudes des pays de l'Union européenne en matière de gestion de l'immigration clandestine, Claude Guéant n'hésite pas à se rendre dans la zone frontalière entre Menton et Vintimille le 4 mars 2011 afin de prendre la mesure du problème

6. Texte de présentation diffusé en service de presse autour de livre de Jean Raspail, *Le Camp des saints* (Paris: Robert Laffont, 1973).

7. « Dossier immigration: serons-nous encore français dans 30 ans? », *Le Figaro magazine*, 26 octobre 1985, 123–132.

8. Dans un article intitulé « Immigration ou invasion » paru dans *Le Figaro Magazine*, 21 septembre 1991, 48–57, Valéry Giscard d'Estaing écrit: « Le type de problème auquel nous aurons à faire face se déplace de celui de l'immigration [...] vers celui de l'invasion » (p. 50).

9. Voir notamment Renaud Camus, *Le Grand Remplacement* (Neuilly-sur-Seine: David Reinharc, 2011).

et de rassurer les Français en réaffirmant sa volonté d'intensifier les reconduites à la frontière.

À la faveur d'une actualité que la France a déjà connu ces dernières années avec l'arrivée de nombreux ressortissants algériens fuyant la guerre civile qui sévit dans leur pays aux années quatre-vingt-dix ou l'affaire de *L'East Sea*, embarcation transportant 908 *boat people* kurdes échouée à Saint-Raphaël en février 2001, ou encore de l'arrivée de 124 réfugiés syriens et irakiens sur les plages de Bonifacio en janvier 2010 sur un bateau de fortune, la vieille antienne de l'invasion de la France par les étrangers retrouve de la vigueur.

Du fantasme de l'invasion à la question de l'identité nationale, il n'y a qu'un pas: inéluctablement depuis trente ans la vie publique est rythmée par un débat sur l'identité nationale protéiforme. Bien souvent ce débat surgit autour des questions liées à l'immigration et l'intégration, même si parfois il se développe sur d'autres terrains comme le genre (par exemple le mariage pour tous).

Avant les années quatre-vingt, d'autres débats sur l'identité nationale ont pu exister: ainsi l'Affaire Dreyfus peut être relue dans cette perspective tant les passions françaises s'y sont reflétées autour du thème de la discrimination, même si la question n'était pas alors posée en ces termes. Toutefois, ce sont bien les années 1980 qui apparaissent comme un tournant dans le rapport de la France à la question de l'immigration devenant un objet de passion publique au point de diviser le pays autour des questions de la tolérance et de l'intégration. Après avoir analysé deux débats lancés aux temps de la « une » du *Figaro Magazine*, nous porterons notre attention sur le premier débat sur l'identité nationale organisé en tant que tel en 2009–2010 sous l'impulsion du président de la République Nicolas Sarkozy.

1- Les premiers débats dans les années quatre-vingt: l'immigration sur la scène médiatique

Au cours de la seconde moitié des années quatre-vingt, deux débats importants, l'un sur le Code de la nationalité et l'autre sur la laïcité suscitent un questionnement global sur l'immigration.

A- « *Qui est Français?* »*: la Commission de la Nationalité en 1987*

Les années quatre-vingt voient les Français indécis et inquiets se diviser sur la définition de la nation et sur les limites de l'appartenance à la communauté des citoyens face à la sédentarisation des populations issues de l'immigration. Une redéfinition des critères d'obtention de la nationalité par une modification du Code de la nationalité en rétrécissant le principe du « droit du sol », qui jusque-là accordait systématiquement la nationalité française aux enfants d'étrangers nés en France, s'est réalisée après deux moments forts de réflexion publique entre 1986 et 1988 puis en 1993. Jusqu'en 1985, l'opinion ignorait tout de l'existence d'un Code de la nationalité. C'est la proposition de modifier des articles réglant les modalités d'accès pour les enfants d'étrangers qui le lui révèle de façon brutale. L'initiative émane de la droite (notamment du RPR) qui l'a inscrite dans son programme pour les élections législatives de 1986.

En quelques années, ce code d'une grande complexité est devenu un détonateur de la vie politique. Ainsi, pendant la première cohabitation entre 1986 et 1988, la contestation de la réforme prévue par le gouvernement Chirac est vive. La proposition d'obliger des jeunes nés en France de parents immigrés à demander la nationalité française au lieu de l'acquérir automatiquement est jugée trop intolérante par des mouvements antiracistes très actifs qui manifestent leur mécontentement sous diverses formes et à plusieurs reprises, ce qui provoque la mise en place d'une commission de « sages » destinée à rendre un avis consultatif dans le but de dépassionner le débat.

Installée par Jacques Chirac le 22 juin 1987, la Commission de la nationalité, composée de spécialistes venus d'horizons divers et présidée par Marceau Long, vice-président du Conseil d'état, siègera plusieurs mois avant de remettre son rapport au Premier ministre le 7 janvier 1988. Son but était d'« [a]pporter une réponse objective et sereine à question d'une éventuelle réforme du droit français de la nationalité, qui avait fait l'objet, au cours des mois ayant précédé son installation, d'un débat trop passionné pour que des options réfléchies et admises par tous puissent être dégagées »[10]. Les travaux comportent trois phases:

–   Du 22 juin au 9 septembre 1987, la Commission s'informe du droit de la nationalité et commence à en discuter. Ses membres reçoivent à plusieurs reprises les magistrats et les hauts fonctionnaires spécialistes des affaires liées à la nationalité.
–   Du 16 septembre au 21 octobre 1987 les auditions publiques, la plupart télévisées en direct, ont lieu (onze séances et cinquante auditions)[11].
–   Du 27 octobre 1987 au 7 janvier 1988, la Commission de la nationalité poursuit ses investigations en privé et élabore un rapport adopté par l'ensemble de ses membres.

La retransmission télévisée en direct des auditions est une manière d'associer les Français aux débats. Pour la première fois dans le pays, une commission nommée par le gouvernement s'informe en direct devant l'opinion publique. Les auditions sont l'occasion d'une vaste réflexion autour de la réforme du Code de la nationalité et au final de l'identité nationale. Tour à tour hauts fonctionnaires, conseillers de l'État, universitaires, responsables d'associations,

---

10. *Être français aujourd'hui et demain*, rapport de la Commission de la nationalité (Paris: Éditions UGE, collection 10/18, 1988).
11. Les auditions se déroulèrent les 16, 18, 24 et 29 septembre 1987, ainsi que les 2, 6, 9, 13, 16 et 21 octobre 1987.

élus, représentants religieux ou personnels de l'Éducation nationale s'expriment sur le sujet.

Des thèmes abordés, qui dépassent souvent le seul accès à la nationalité pour s'élargir à la question plus générale de l'immigration, se dégagent quatre préoccupations principales: l'opportunité de la réforme, l'idée de démarche volontaire des jeunes issus de l'immigration pour devenir effectivement français, la double nationalité et l'intégration. Des opinions émises lors de ces auditions autour du thème de l'intégration ressort la nécessité de transformer les étrangers selon un modèle unique républicain. Mais ce consensus révèle également les difficultés à définir les contours de ce modèle et les façons de le transmettre.

Lorsque Marceau Long remet le résultat des travaux de la Commission au Premier ministre, ce sont 60 propositions, plus libérales dans l'ensemble que le projet de réforme initial. Si la Commission valide la notion selon laquelle la plupart des enfants d'immigrés devraient dorénavant exprimer la volonté d'acquérir la nationalité française au lieu de la recevoir automatiquement, elle fait de nombreuses recommandations conçues pour faciliter cette démarche. Les sages souhaitent que les procédures de naturalisation soient plus rapides et plus transparentes, tout en suggérant d'allonger de six mois à un an le délai d'obtention de la nationalité par mariage tandis que la bi-nationalité des Franco-Algériens n'est pas contestée. Marceau Long présente cet ensemble de propositions comme une réponse sereine à un problème soulevant les passions « dans une conception ambitieuse et optimiste de la France de demain, fidèle en tous cas à la tradition juridique séculaire de notre pays ». Ainsi, on pourrait devenir français plus facilement et plus consciemment. Tandis que son président affirme ne pas souhaiter réduire le nombre des personnes devenant françaises chaque année mais l'augmenter, le grand principe qui guide la Commission consiste avant tout à promouvoir la notion d'intégration.

François Mitterrand réélu en 1988, le débat sur la nationalité s'atténua et le Code resta en l'état. Avec les différents gouvernements socialistes de Michel Rocard (1988–1991), Édith Cresson (1991–1992) et de Pierre Bérégovoy (1992–1993), il est rarement question du Code de la nationalité. En revanche, avec la seconde cohabitation et le gouvernement Balladur, le débat resurgit. La plate-forme de l'Union Pour la France (UPF) qui regroupe RPR et UDF, élaborée dès 1990, avait prévu un chapitre intitulé « Un État qui maîtrise l'immigration » proposant un nouveau projet de réforme du Code de la nationalité permettant au futur gouvernement de clarifier les conditions de l'intégration et d'appartenance nationale. Dans cette optique, le renforcement de l'identité nationale passe par la limitation voire la suppression du droit du sol.

La victoire de la droite aux élections législatives de 1993 est écrasante et très vite, le gouvernement Balladur fait de la gestion de l'immigration sa première préoccupation. Pour défendre l'identité nationale il faut mettre en œuvre des mesures restrictives dont la réforme du Code de la nationalité. Ce projet ne provoque plus guère de remous étant donné les circonstances politiques favorables à la droite, et, contrairement à 1986–87, l'opposition de gauche et antiraciste n'est plus en mesure de mobiliser l'opinion.

B- L'affaire du voile en 1989: la laïcité en péril?

Entre octobre et décembre 1989, alors que tombe le Mur de Berlin, la France se passionne avec une intensité sans précédent pour un fait divers qui touche directement à la question de l'immigration en lien avec l'École et plus encore les valeurs de l'identité nationale. Le 4 octobre 1989, trois jeunes filles de confession musulmane sont renvoyées du collège Havez de Creil (Oise) parce qu'elles persistent à porter le foulard islamique malgré l'interdiction du Principal. Cette attitude leur vaut d'être provisoirement exclues de l'établissement.

Très vite le débat dépasse la question du règlement de ce fait divers et même la seule question de l'islam en France: les principes fondamentaux d'organisation de la société française sont mis en cause, liant les questions de l'immigration, de la laïcité, d'accueil des étrangers, du droit à la différence. Les antagonismes dépassent les clivages politiques traditionnels.

Pourtant l'incident semble clos dès le 10 octobre. En effet, un compromis est trouvé entre le Principal du collège, Ernest Chenière, et les trois collégiennes: elles pourront porter le foulard sauf dans les salles de classe où elles le poseront sur leurs épaules. Mais les adolescentes rompent le pacte dix jours plus tard ce qui les amène à être une nouvelle fois exclues. Et c'est à partir du 20 octobre que le véritable débat s'engage, lorsque deux personnalités importantes prennent position en faveur de l'acceptation du voile. Le 23 octobre, dans un communiqué à la presse, l'épouse du président de la République, Danielle Mitterrand, se prononce contre l'exclusion des jeunes filles ce qui provoque une volée de critiques. Puis le 25 octobre, c'est au tour du ministre de l'Éducation nationale, Lionel Jospin, interpellé à l'Assemblée nationale de déclarer qu'on devait accueillir les jeunes filles qui persistaient à porter ce foulard: « L'École ne peut exclure car elle est faite pour accueillir ». Le Premier ministre Michel Rocard apporte un soutien timide à Lionel Jospin le 5 novembre. Quand au président de la République, il reste longtemps silencieux avant d'accorder son soutien à Lionel Jospin le 23 novembre 1989. Les vacances de la Toussaint ne calment pas la polémique: le débat alimenté quotidiennement se prolonge encore un mois jusqu'à ce que le Conseil d'État, sollicité par le ministre de l'Éducation nationale, ne rende son avis le 27 novembre. Les sages donnent raison au ministre en restant toutefois mitigés: le port d'insignes religieux par les élèves n'est pas incompatible avec le principe de laïcité, à condition toutefois que ces signes ne revêtent pas un « caractère ostentatoire ou revendicatif ».

Dans la pratique cela revient à faire régler la question au cas par cas par les chefs d'établissement: ces affaires devront se résoudre dans un contexte local et non national, de sorte qu'il n'est pas encore question d'une loi à ce sujet. Lionel Jospin, dans une circulaire du 6 décembre, laisse ainsi le soin aux directeurs d'établissement de régler les affaires de foulard. Dès lors le débat perd de son intensité avant de ressurgir en 1994 et à nouveau en 2003.

En se référant aux controverses soulevées par le port du foulard à l'école, les médias parleront souvent – et non sans une certaine ambiguïté – de « l'affaire du voile ». Jusqu'alors le terme « voile islamique » avait été couramment entendu comme désignant un morceau d'étoffe recouvrant le visage d'une femme, à l'instar de l'image publiée sur la une du *Figaro magazine* en octobre 1985. À partir de l'affaire de 1989, les mots « voile » et « tchador » sont utilisés par les médias pour désigner une large gamme de tenues vestimentaires islamiques couvrant dans certains cas uniquement les cheveux, dans d'autres cas les cheveux et tout le visage en dehors des yeux, et dans d'autres cas encore l'ensemble de la tête ainsi que d'autres parties du corps.

Quoi qu'il en soit, l'affaire du voile révèle l'existence de deux conceptions antagonistes de la laïcité: l'une rigide et fermée à toute évolution au nom de sa vocation universelle; l'autre, plus souple se voulant tolérante et évolutive, opposition qui, là encore, ne recoupe pas les clivages traditionnels. Dans les deux cas, le statut de l'immigré et son intégration à la société française est l'enjeu majeur puisqu'il s'agit de faire coïncider des traditions religieuses souvent perçues comme communautaires avec l'École laïque. Pour tous, la priorité se situe dans la défense de la laïcité et dans le refus d'un quelconque prosélytisme religieux. Le voile est-il signe ou non de prosélytisme? De leur côté, les arguments des tenants d'une laïcité rigide s'ordonnent autour de quatre idées principales confortée par l'affaire du voile: les principes républicains et laïques sont intouchables; les comportements au sein de l'école doivent être uniformes; l'intégrisme musulman, associé à tort ou à raison avec le port du voile, est déstabilisateur et la tolérance envers des modes de vie différents est limitée. Les opposants à l'exclusion des jeunes filles voilées sont minoritaires entre octobre et novembre 1989: ils argumentent leur position en critiquant les positions frileuses des partisans d'une laïcité intransigeante, en favorisant le dialogue et la dédramatisation, et en provoquant une prise de conscience du métissage de la société française.

En tout cas derrière le voile se pose la question de l'immigration, de l'intégration et de la société multiculturelle et le débat, jamais réellement clos, ne va cesser de rebondir jusqu'à nos jours. Il devient un débat autour de la place de l'islam en France, régulièrement alimenté dans les médias et dans la classe politique.

L'un des temps de réflexion les plus significatifs se situe en 2003 avec les travaux de la Commission Stasi dans un contexte de polémiques sur la question du voile islamique à l'école et la nécessité ou non de faire une loi interdisant le port de signes religieux en milieu scolaire. Installée le 3 juillet 2003 par le président de la République Jacques Chirac qui souhaite un temps de réflexion, la Commission est composée de 20 membres autour de Bernard Stasi (1930–2011), médiateur de la République. Pendant trois mois, elle auditionne quelque 140 personnes représentant la société civile, les partis politiques et les instances religieuses du pays, dont une centaine en séance publique. Lors de la remise officielle de ce rapport, le 17 décembre 2003, le président Chirac demande aux Français de se rassembler autour du principe de laïcité, « pierre angulaire de la République, faisceau de nos valeurs communes de respect, de tolérance, de dialogue »[12]. Appelant à des accommodements raisonnables, le rapport défend deux principes majeurs: la neutralité de l'État, qui impose à la République d'assurer « l'égalité devant la loi de tous les citoyens sans distinction d'origine, de race ou de religion », et la liberté de conscience avec notamment sa déclinaison en liberté de culte. Elle relève que des tensions peuvent apparaître entre ces deux pôles que sont la neutralité de l'État laïque et la liberté de conscience, notamment dans son expression religieuse; les cadres de ces tensions sont principalement l'armée, la prison, l'hôpital et l'école[13]. Parmi la douzaine de recommandations proposées dans le rapport, une seule sera mise en œuvre par le Président Chirac qui fera voter par le Parlement en 2004 une loi interdisant le port de tout signe religieux jugé « ostensible » à l'école publique. Cette interdiction du foulard en milieu scolaire, prônée par la Commission Stasi, sera complétée en 2010 par une loi interdisant la dissimulation du visage dans tout espace public et non plus seulement à l'école, qui vise notamment à réprimer le port de la burqa.

2- L'identité nationale, un débat mis en scène sous Sarkozy en 2009–10

Mettant à exécution une volonté présidentielle formulée lors de la campagne électorale de Nicolas Sarkozy en 2007, le ministre de l'Immigration, Éric Besson, invité du Grand Jury RTL-Le Figaro-LCI le 25 octobre 2009, annonce un vaste débat sur l'identité nationale: « J'ai envie de lancer un grand débat sur les valeurs de l'identité nationale, sur ce qu'est être Français aujourd'hui »[14].

Si, comme nous venons de le voir, ce débat est loin d'être une nouveauté, l'inédit réside dans la forme: pour la première fois, un gouvernement décide de son propre chef d'organiser un débat directement sur ce thème. À dessein, la mise en place du ministère de l'Immigration, de l'Intégration, de l'Identité nationale et du Co-développement d'abord confié à Brice Hortefeux entre mai 2007 et janvier 2009 puis à Éric Besson entre janvier 2009 et la fin de ce ministère en novembre 2010, porte cette ambition de débattre directement d'un sujet majeur avec le but

---

12. *Libération*, 18 décembre 2003.

13. Voir le rapport Stasi en ligne sur le site de *La Documentation française* < http://www.ladocumentationfrancaise.fr/var/storage/rapports-publics/034000725.pdf> [consulté le 9 juin 2015].

14. *Le Monde,* 26 octobre 2009.

de « réaffirmer la fierté d'être français ». Mais, au-delà du débat formaté par le gouvernement, le questionnement sur l'identité nationale ne cesse de se poser de manière répétitive. Il se fixe en particulier sur la place de l'islam en France, question traumatisante posée depuis plusieurs décennies[15]. Particularité du quinquennat Sarkozy, la peur de l'islam se décline autour d'un nouvel habit: le voile intégral ou burqa.

A – Un débat organisé par l'État

Avec cette consultation tous azimuts, Éric Besson relance de manière spectaculaire l'un des thèmes les plus porteurs de la campagne électorale de Nicolas Sarkozy[16]. D'ailleurs, le président de la République, en déplacement dans le Vercors pour inaugurer le Mémorial de La Chapelle-en-Vercors, le 11 novembre 2009, apporte sa caution au débat, tenant à balayer les suspicions: « Parler d'identité nationale n'est pas dangereux mais nécessaire, car la France doute d'elle-même »[17].

Le débat proposé par Éric Besson s'étire sur plusieurs mois entre le début de novembre 2009 et février 2010. Le Ministre, comme aux temps du Second Empire à propos d'autres questions, décide de solliciter préfets et sous-préfets afin qu'ils organisent des réunions avec les « forces vives de la Nation » sur le thème « qu'est-ce qu'être Français? Quelles sont les valeurs qui nous relient? Quelle est la nature du lien qui fait que nous sommes français et que nous devons être fiers? ». Justifiant sa démarche Éric Besson estime qu'il faut « réaffirmer les valeurs de l'identité nationale et la fierté d'être français ».[18]

Une semaine seulement après son lancement, le succès semble au rendez-vous: le site dédié, debatidentitenationale.fr[19], reçoit plus de 185.000 visites et 25.000 contributions sont déposées en réponse à la question « pour vous, qu'est-ce qu'être Français? ». Au total, 58.000 contributions seront relevées en février 2010[20]. Des réunions, ouvertes aux Français comme aux étrangers, sont

---

15. Voir Gilles Kepel, *Les Banlieues de l'Islam: naissance d'une religion en France* (Paris: Le Seuil, 1987) et Bruno Étienne, *L'Islam en France: état et société* (Paris: Éditions du Centre National de la Recherche Scientifique, 1990).

16. En effet, peu avant l'élection présidentielle de 2007, un sondage CSA-Cisco pour France 3 et France Info avait fait apparaître que 62% des Français et surtout 81% des électeurs potentiels de Nicolas Sarkozy pensaient que placer le thème de l'identité nationale dans le débat électoral était une « bonne chose ».

17. *Le Journal du Dimanche*, 12 novembre 2009.

18. *Le Monde*, 25 octobre 2009.

19. Ce site n'est plus accessible.

20. Lors d'une conférence de presse sous la forme d'un bilan d'étape, le 3 janvier 2010, Éric Besson, avec Brice Teinturier, directeur général adjoint de l'Institut TNS-SOFRES, présente une analyse lexicale de la moitié des contributions postées ainsi qu'une analyse « qualitative » de 500 d'entre elles en cherchant à révéler la richesse des contributions.

organisées au niveau local dans l'ensemble des départements de la France métropolitaine et dans les départements et territoires d'Outre-Mer[21]. Un sondage commandé à l'institut TNS-Sofres par le ministère de l'Immigration de l'Intégration, de l'Identité nationale et du Co-développement en janvier 2010 révèle que l'identité nationale existe pour 82% des Français interrogés même si parmi eux, 74% estiment qu'elle a « tendance à s'affaiblir ». Mais cela n'empêche pas 75% des sondés de s'estimer « fiers d'être français »[22].

Cette vaste réflexion autour des éléments concrets du « vivre ensemble » donne une photographie de la manière dont une certaine France envisage le rapport à l'Autre au tournant de la décennie et au cœur du quinquennat. Parmi les propositions d'action, beaucoup s'orientent d'une part vers le principe d'un nécessaire respect des valeurs françaises: renforcer le contrat d'accueil et d'intégration, augmenter le niveau de connaissance de la langue française, faire de l'entretien d'assimilation préalable un temps fort du processus de naturalisation. D'autre part, il en résulte que la « fierté d'être Français » doit être réaffirmée en offrant davantage de place aux symboles de la République (drapeau tricolore, *Marseillaise*, buste de Marianne, sigle RF) dans l'espace public et organisant, localement et avec une certaine solennité, des cycles de conférences d'instruction civique et « citoyenne » ouverts à tous[23].

B - Un forum tronqué?

Cependant, force est de constater que le grand débat voulu par Éric Besson, bien qu'approuvé par une majorité de Français[24], n'obtient pas les résultats escomptés. Son ambition médiatique de présenter une majorité gouvernementale décomplexée sur l'immigration et posant « les vrais problèmes » face à une

---

Voir *Libération*, 4 janvier 2010 et voir le site de TNS-SOFRES, 4 janvier 2010, « *"Pour vous qu'est-ce qu'être Français?"*, analyse des contributions au site dédié au débat sur l'identité nationale ». Les commentaires considérés comme « déchets » comprenant aussi bien des propos « hors sujet » que « racistes ou xénophobes » n'ont pas été pris en compte. Selon le Ministère, ils représentent environ 15% des contributions totales. Éric Besson ne précise pas qu'une censure a été exercée: dès novembre certaines contributions d'internautes très critiques envers le gouvernement ou trop violemment racistes n'ont pas été publiés sur le site officiel. Voir sur ce sujet, le site des décodeurs du blog du *Monde* < http://decodeurs.blog.lemonde.fr/2010/01/07/identite-nationale-le-debat-sest-bien-focalise-sur-limmigration/ > [consulté le 9 juin 2015].

21. Au moins une réunion est organisée et animée à l'initiative du Corps préfectoral dans chacun des 342 arrondissements français. D'autres réunions sont organisées plus spon-tanément à l'initiative de parlementaires, élus locaux, mouvements associatifs, enseig-nants ou parents d'élèves, représentants des cultes, etc.

22. *L'Express,* 5 février 2010.

23. *Le Monde*, 9 février 2010.

24. *Le Parisien*, 1er novembre 2009, sondage réalisé par CSA indiquant que 60 % des per-sonnes interrogées approuvent l'organisation d'un tel débat.

opposition de gauche embarrassée et une extrême droite concurrencée sur son propre terrain a fait long feu. Après quelques semaines, la mécanique subit de nombreux faux-pas et dérapages.

Loin de susciter l'engouement populaire, les débats organisés sous le contrôle des préfets avec pas mal d'incertitudes et de confusion comme le montre la circulaire du 2 novembre 2009 envoyée par le ministère aux préfets qui surprend par son manque de cadrage et de rigueur, malgré quelques succès ponctuels comme à Sarcelles, n'attirent qu'une faible assistance et surtout pas de jeunes[25]. Pire, les rares présents n'hésitent pas, dans des ambiances souvent houleuses, à tenir des propos bien souvent teintés de racisme tel cet homme au Raincy: « Je me sens saturé dans les bus, je suis le seul Gaulois blanc! » ou un autre à Wailly-Beaucamp: « Il ne faut pas confondre l'immigration polonaise et celle venant d'autres continents. Je vais rester politiquement correct... Mais les Polonais n'ont jamais brûlé de drapeau français »[26]. Parfois les dérapages pouvaient venir des hommes politiques eux-mêmes tel Jean-Claude Gaudin, lors du débat organisé à Marseille le 14 janvier 2010, déclarant au sujet d'un match qualificatif pour la Coupe du Monde de football et gagné par l'Algérie: « Nous nous réjouissons que les Musulmans soient heureux du résultat, sauf que quand après ils déferlent à 15.000 ou à 20.000 sur la Canebière, il n'y a que le drapeau algérien et il n'y a pas le drapeau français, cela ne nous plaît pas »[27].

Discrédité par les oppositions de l'extrême gauche au Front national, refusant la plupart du temps de prendre part aux discussions qualifiées de « mascarades »[28] destinées à récupérer les voix des électeurs d'extrême droite à quelques mois des régionales[29], le débat ne se déroule généralement pas dans des conditions satisfaisantes et se transforme parfois en foire d'empoigne xénophobe. D'autant que, progressivement, la majorité se divise: les plus lucides, tels Alain Juppé, Jean-Pierre Raffarin, Dominique De Villepin ou François Baroin, expriment tout haut leurs doutes sur cette « équipée ».

En lançant le débat sur l'identité nationale, Éric Besson a ainsi « ouvert la boîte de Pandore » comme le note Thierry Leclère dans *Télérama*: « La question

25. *Libération,* 4 décembre 2009, éditorial de Laurent Joffrin « Identité nationale: le débat dérape ».

26. *Libération*, 5 janvier 2010, « Débat sur l'identité nationale: le vrai bilan et la carte des ratés ».

27. L'*Express,* 17 janvier 2010 « Le débat sur l'identité nationale dénoncé après le dérapage de Jean-Claude Gaudin ».

28. *L'Humanité*, 18 janvier 2010, « Une mascarade nauséabonde ».

29. *Le Journal Du Dimanche,* 29 novembre 2009. Une enquête d'opinion, réalisée par l'IFOP en novembre 2009, indique que pour une large majorité de Français (72%), le débat sur l'identité nationale voulu par le gouvernement constitue avant tout « une stratégie pour gagner les élections régionales » de mars 2010.

de l'identité nationale vire au défouloir raciste »[30]. Les discussions, focalisées sur l'immigration, ont mis en lumière les fantasmes et les tourments de l'opinion française. L'émission d'Arlette Chabot À vous de juger, programmée le 13 janvier 2010 symbolise les termes du débat: Éric Besson y affronte Marine Le Pen alors vice-présidente du Front national, dans une ambiance tendue, sans enthousiasme ni relief et sur fond de polémique[31].

Après trois mois de débat et autant de polémique, à la demande du président Sarkozy, le premier ministre François Fillon organise le 8 février 2010 à l'hôtel de Matignon un séminaire intergouvernemental afin d'annoncer des mesures concrètes, préalablement envisagée par le ministre de l'Immigration. Il décide de mettre en place une Commission de personnalités composée de parlementaires, intellectuels et historiens, pour « approfondir le sujet » et surtout pour mettre ainsi un terme à ce débat devenu bien embarrassant[32]. D'autre part, alors qu'Éric Besson ponctue à sa manière la réflexion par l'animation d'un colloque organisé le 8 avril à Paris sur le thème « Identités nationales, identité européenne » en présence de ministres et d'intellectuels européens[33], le président Sarkozy se charge à son tour de clore le débat à Chambéry, le 22 avril, à l'occasion de la commémoration du cent cinquantième anniversaire du rattachement de la Savoie à la France en vantant... l'identité savoyarde. Nicolas Sarkozy déclare: « L'unité de la France a plus à craindre d'une uniformité rigide que d'une souplesse dans la diversité et la reconnaissance de chacune des identités de notre territoire. On ne bâtit pas un grand pays en niant les identités de toutes ses petites patries qui font la patrie française »[34].

Proposer une identité nationale, entre identité européenne et identité régionale, telle est la manière plutôt inattendue de sortir d'une polémique qui aurait pu être évitée[35]. La gauche ironise en estimant que « la montagne à accouché d'une souris », comme le note François Hollande pour le Parti Socialiste sur son blog: « pourquoi fallait-il déchaîner tant de passions, provoquer tant de dérapages, susciter tant de légitimes suspicions, pour finir par apposer une Déclaration des droits de l'homme dans chaque classe, ou faire chanter une fois par an la Marseillaise à chaque jeune Français, sans que l'on sache très bien si ceux qui ne le sont pas devraient également entonner l'hymne national »[36]. L'analyse délivrée

---

30. *Télérama*, 9 février 2010.
31. *Libération,* 14 janvier 2010.
32. *Le Monde*, 8 et 9 février 2010, « Débat sur l'identité nationale: bon débarras! ».
33. *Le Monde*, 7–8 mars et *Le Point*, 8 avril 2010.
34. *Le Journal du Dimanche*, 25 avril 2010, « Sarkozy vante l'identité savoyarde ».
35. Un sondage, révèle que 63 % des Français estiment que le débat n'a pas été constructif tandis que 61% jugent qu'il n'a pas permis de définir ce qu'était « être Français »; cf. *20 Minutes*, 1er février 2010.
36. *Le Monde*, 8 février 2010.

par Jean-Luc Mélenchon pour le Front de Gauche sur *France info* va dans le même sens: « Bon débarras! Ça suffit! Il faut parler d'autre chose parce que de toute façon, ça ne pouvait déboucher sur rien. Tout ça est une comédie sinistre et de nombreux Français doivent ressentir un grand dégoût d'avoir vu une telle débauche d'histoires de fous déclenchées dans ce pays pour rien »[37].

Symptomatique d'un air du temps inquiet sur l'avenir de la France, l'exposition très médiatique du thème de l'identité nationale, voulue par le Président Sarkozy n'a pas fait avancer un questionnement qui taraude la France depuis trois décennies. Ce nouvel épisode, original et spectaculaire, a plutôt révélé l'impossibilité de mettre en place sereinement un débat aussi complexe et difficile dans un cadre aussi formaté: libérer la parole, c'est s'exposer à un racisme ordinaire qui a débordé les promoteurs de ce vaste forum national. Il confirme également la stratégie médiatique de Nicolas Sarkozy, tentant d'utiliser le thème de l'immigration pour améliorer son image.

Conclusion

Les attentats de janvier 2015 ont été suivis par d'immenses rassemblements, notamment à Paris, au nom de l'union nationale. Ces manifestations d'unité face au terrorisme djihadiste ne font que suspendre très provisoirement les tensions identitaires qui ne cessent d'agiter la sphère publique. Les minorités stigmatisées à maintes reprises au cours des débats qui ont marqué les décennies précédentes brillent par leur quasi-absence des rassemblements censés incarner l'unité nationale. Hormis la multiplication de dispositions sécuritaires et de références incantatoires aux vertus de la laïcité, les mesures proposées pour combler les fractures ethniques et sociales qui ont nourri la violence des extrémistes sont bien maigres. En l'absence de mesures visant à réduire les inégalités et les discriminations qui sévissent sur le terrain, les débats qui depuis trente ans font rage autour du thème de l'identité nationale semblent avoir finalement trop peu apporté à la construction d'une véritable unité de la nation.

---

37. *Libération*, 9 février 2010.

Nottingham French Studies 54.3 (2015): 297–311
DOI: 10.3366/nfs.2015.0128
© University of Nottingham
www.euppublishing.com/journal/nfs

FRENCH CINEMA AND THE INTEGRATION OF YOUNG WOMEN ACTORS OF MAGHREBI HERITAGE

CARRIE TARR

Introduction

In the early years of the twenty-first century there has been a notable shift in the presence and status of ethnic minority actors in French cinema. In the last two decades of the twentieth century, as scholars such as Guy Austin, Ginette Vincendeau and Will Higbee have indicated, cinematic stardom in France signally failed to reflect the multi-ethnic composition of its postcolonial population.[1] Actors of Maghrebi origin, if they managed to find parts in mainstream French cinema, tended to be confined to marginalized and/or stereotypical roles, contributing to the dominant media construction of ethnic others as deviants and/or outsiders, be it as criminals or prostitutes in crime films or as the victims of white racism in more concerned liberal, white-authored dramas.[2] Even in the group of films made in the 1980s and 1990s that have come to be known as 'cinéma beur'[3], that is films foregrounding the subjectivities of young people of Maghrebi origin born and brought up in France, ethnic minority actors did not find roles that gave them star status. The most illustrious exception is perhaps Smaïn,[4] a comic actor whose celebrity was enhanced by his performance in

1. See Guy Austin, *Stars in Modern French Film* (London: Arnold, 2003); Ginette Vincendeau, *Stars and Stardom in French Cinema* (London and New York: Continuum, 2000); Will Higbee, *Post-Beur Cinema: North African Émigré and Maghrebi-French Filmaking in France since 2000* (Edinburgh: Edinburgh University Press, 2013).

2. See Carrie Tarr, *Reframing Difference: 'Beur' and 'Banlieue' Filmmaking in France* (Manchester and New York: Manchester University Press, 2005), pp. 9–10.

3. See Tarr, *Reframing Difference*; Higbee, *Post-Beur Cinema*.

4. Although global French star Isabelle Adjani acknowledged her ethnic heritage (an Algerian father, a German mother) in the mid-1980s, her star ethnicity has remained largely 'of the unmarked kind: visible whiteness, stellar luminescence' (Austin, *Stars in Modern French Film*, p. 105). In the 2009 TV drama *La Journée de la jupe* (Jean-Paul Lilienfeld), however, she plays a French literature teacher who eventually reveals her Maghrebi origin. See Geneviève Sellier, 'Don't touch the white woman: *La Journée de la jupe* or Feminism at the Service of Islamophobia', in *Screening Integration: Recasting Maghrebi Immigration in Contemporary France*, ed. by Sylvie Durmelat and Vinay Swamy (Lincoln, NE and London: University of Nebraska Press, 2011), pp. 144–60.

Serge Meynard's *L'Œil au beur(re) noir* (1987), pointing not just to the significance of comedy as a vehicle for stardom in France, as Vincendeau has demonstrated,[5] but also to the failure of French celebrity culture of the period to accommodate more than a token representative of France's postcolonial others.

However, over the last fifteen years or so, a remarkable change has taken place, a change which can perhaps be traced back to the success of Mathieu Kassovitz's *La Haine* (1995), which catapulted the roles of ethnic minority youths from the French *banlieue* into the limelight, but may also be linked to the growth of multiplex cinemas in the *banlieue* and hence to the growth of a multi-ethnic audience.[6] Increasing numbers of box-office hits (films with over a million spectators) have since centred on France as a multi-ethnic, multicultural society, providing a variety of roles in both genre and auteur films which have enabled ethnic minority actors not only to play leading roles but to reach the pinnacle of the French star system. The five most successful stars of Maghrebi heritage to date are: Samy Naceri (co-star of the *Taxi* series which began in 1998 and produced three sequels), Jamel Debbouze (star of Djamel Bensalah's *Le Ciel, les oiseaux, . . . et ta mère!* in 1999 and then Alain Chabat's *Astérix et Obélix: Mission Cléopâtre* in 2002), Gad Elmaleh (who joined the successful team of Thomas Gilou's *La Vérité si je mens* series in 2001 and had a huge hit with Merzak Allouache's *Chouchou* in 2003), and Dany Boon and Kad Merad (who achieved megastardom with Boon's *Bienvenue chez les Ch'tis* in 2008).[7] One might also note the consecration of French actors of Maghrebi heritage when the Cannes Best Actor award of 2006 went collectively to Debbouze, Naceri, Roschdy Zem and Sami Bouajila (together with white French actor Bernard Blancan), for their roles in Rachid Bouchareb's highly successful historical drama *Indigènes/Days of Glory,* which traces the hitherto unrecognized role of North African soldiers in the liberation of France in the Second World War.

What is noticeable about these examples, however, is not only the importance of comedy, and the ability of the actors in question to play both ethnically marked and unmarked roles, but also the fact that these stars are all male. While this may in part be due to French audiences' preference for comedies which are largely a

---

5.   Ginette Vincendeau, 'From the Margins to the Center, French Stardom and Ethnicity', in *A Companion to Contemporary French Cinema*, ed. by Alistair Fox, Michel Marie, Raphaëlle Moine and Hilary Radner (Hoboken, NJ: John Wiley, 2015), pp. 541–69.

6.   See Alec Hargreaves, 'Les Trois Âges cinématographiques des Maghrébins en France', in *Images et représentations des Maghrébins dans le cinéma en France* (*Migrance*, 37:1 (2011)), 99–100.

7.   Of these, Naceri, Boon and Merad are of mixed Franco-Algerian parentage, while Gad Elmaleh is of Moroccan Jewish origin. More recently Omar Sy has become the first black French actor of African heritage to reach megastardom, as the co-star of Eric Toledano and Olivier Nakache's 2011 hit *Intouchables*.

male-oriented genre, there are no doubt other factors at stake. If, as Geneviève Sellier argues, 'French actresses [sic] are seen principally to incarnate sexuality, whereas the image of male actors is much richer and more socially and culturally complex',[8] then the roles enabling female actors to construct a distinctive star image will be proportionately fewer. Furthermore, the fact that fewer women than men, and disproportionately even fewer ethnic minority women than ethnic minority men, have gained access to filmmaking[9] may mean even fewer opportunities for female ethnic minority actors to make an impact, since it is primarily women directors who foreground socially and culturally complex roles for ethnic minority women.[10] Even so, feature films by the most prominent French women directors of Maghrebi origin, Zaïda Ghorab-Volta, Yamina Benguigui and Rachida Krim (and more recently Reem Kherici with her 2013 comedy, *Paris à tout prix*), though they may feature strong female ethnic minority characters and contribute to the feminization of a cinematic space which has otherwise largely been considered the location for the expression of troubled, masculine postcolonial identities, have not produced roles which have propelled their female actors to the height of stardom.[11]

Nevertheless, since the turn of the century, for the first time three young female ethnic minority actors have achieved the award of Most Promising Newcomer (Meilleur espoir féminin) at the industry's annual César ceremonies in films which have achieved significant popular and/or critical success while foregrounding the role of a young French woman of Maghrebi heritage. In 2002, it was awarded to Rachida Brakni for her performance in Coline Serreau's *Chaos* (2001; 1,161,494 spectators in France),[12] in 2008 to Hafsia Herzi for her performance in Abdellatif Kechiche's *La Graine et le mulet/Couscous* (2007; 892,684 spectators in France), and in 2011 to Leïla Bekhti for her performance in

---

8. See Sellier, 'Don't touch the white woman', p. 153.

9. Only four films of the decade 2000–2010, less than 1%, were directed by French women of Maghrebi heritage. See Carrie Tarr, 'Introduction: Women's Film-making in France 2000–2010', *Studies in French Cinema*, 12:3 (2012), 189–200 (p. 192).

10. Exceptions include films by male directors of Maghrebi origin such as *Douce France* (Malik Chibane, 1995) and *L'Esquive* (Abdellatif Kechiche, 2004) and white French film-maker Philippe Faucon's *Samia* (2001) and *Dans la vie* (2008).

11. See Carrie Tarr, 'Le Rôle des femmes dans le cinéma des réalisatrices d'origine magh-rébine en France 1980–2010', in *Images et représentations des Maghrébins dans le cinéma en France* (*Migrance*, 37:1 (2011)), 47–53. For a discussion of the role of women in a wider range of films, see Patricia Geesey, 'A Space of their Own? Women in Maghrebi-French Filmmaking', in Durmelat and Swamy (eds), *Screening Integration*, pp. 161–77.

12. Box office figures for France are taken from the LUMIERE database which provides a compilation of data on admissions of films released in European cinemas since 1996. See < http://lumiere.obs.coe.int/web/search/> [last accessed 25 May 2015].

Tout ce qui brille/All That Glitters (2010; 1,439,624 spectators in France), a first film by Géraldine Nakache and Hervé Mimran. On the assumption that this award may be indicative of the growing visibility and acceptance of Maghrebi-French female actors at the centre rather than the periphery of the French film industry, this article focuses on the career trajectories of these three young actors and their contribution to the representation of gender, ethnicity and identity in contemporary multi-ethnic postcolonial France. It examines first the roles that thrust them into the limelight, then the subsequent progress of their careers, both in France and in a transnational context, before attempting to assess whether the promise of national stardom indicated by the César awards has been vindicated.

Award-winning roles in *Chaos*, *Couscous* and *All That Glitters*
Rachida Brakni, who was born in 1977 in Paris to Algerian immigrant parents and enjoyed a classical training as an actor, first at the Studio-Théâtre of Asnières-sur-Seine, then at the Conservatoire national supérieur d'art dramatique in Paris, began her acting career at the Comédie-Française, following in the steps of Isabelle Adjani, where she won a Molière for her role in *Ruy Blas* in 1997. Her break-through role into cinema came with Coline Serreau's feminist comedy thriller *Chaos* in which she plays Noémie/Malika, a prostitute of Maghrebi origin, who escapes her situation thanks to the friendship of Hélène (Catherine Frot), a middle-class white French woman who witnesses her being viciously beaten up and left in a coma by her pimps and helps her not only to escape, but also to rescue her sister from the forced marriage being planned by her immigrant Maghrebi family.[13] Breaking away from the type of token role accorded to the 'beurette de service' and subverting the stereotype of the 'sexy beurette',[14] Brakni embodies Noémie/Malika not only as an action heroine who organizes the downfall of her former pimps, but also as a brilliant financier capable of successfully playing the stock exchange, and as a feminist avenger who seduces and discards Hélène's husband and son in order to teach them what misogynists they are. The film ends, if ambiguously, with a shot grouping Noémie/Malika and Hélène with Malika's sister and Hélène's put-upon mother-in-law in the grounds of a villa overlooking the sea purchased by Malika, offering a feminist message of cross-cultural and intergenerational female solidarity and independence that is achieved largely thanks to Malika's lucidity, drive and organizational skills. The film thus uses Brakni to construct an image of the young woman of Maghrebi origin as an enterprising, upwardly mobile, intelligent and hard-edged but

---

13. For a detailed analysis of *Chaos*, see Tarr, *Reframing Difference*, pp. 153–66.
14. See Nacera Guénif Souilamas, *Des 'beurettes' aux descendantes d'immigrants nord-africains* (Paris: Bernard Grasset, 2000).

seductive, westernized feminist, a complex image that Brakni has both traded on and modified in her subsequent career.[15]

Hafsia Herzi, born in 1987 in Manosque and brought up in Marseille by parents of Tunisian and Algerian heritage, had an early minor role in a French TV adaptation of a novel by Marcel Pagnol. However, her first major acting role was in *Couscous*, a social realist family drama set in the port town of Sète. As Rym, a passionate, loyal and determined young woman of Maghrebi heritage, she assists her stepfather, Slimane (the central character), in his project of setting up a restaurant on an old converted boat after he has been made redundant from his work at the docks. Her affectionate encouragement of Slimane includes on the one hand her accompanying him to the bank to help him ask for a loan, on the other spontaneously performing a belly dance, at great length, at the gala evening he has organized for potential sponsors, in order to placate the expectant guests when she realizes the couscous they need to serve has gone missing. Although this scene has been criticized as offering a stereotypical representation of the 'sexy beurette' as object of the gaze, arguably it functions rather to discomfort the spectator who is obliged to watch Rym/Herzi knowingly fulfil that role in order to conform to the primarily white French guests' expectations.[16] At the same time, the film's emphasis on the body and her role as devoted helpmate to an older man has perhaps made it more difficult for Herzi subsequently to break away from sexualized, subordinate roles.

Unlike Brakni, whose earlier career lay in the theatre, and Herzi, who was undertaking her first major acting role, Leïla Bekhti already had a significant body of work behind her, both in film and in television, before her award-winning performance in *All That Glitters*. Born in 1984 in Issy-les-Moulineaux to immigrant Algerian parents, she studied drama at school and made her debut in a small role in Kim Chaperon's horror film *Sheïtan* (2006), starring Vincent Cassel, and in Gurinder Chadha's contribution to the collective film *Paris, je t'aime* (2006), as well as getting a more significant part in Roschdy Zem's first film as director, *Mauvaise foi* (2006), in which she plays Mounia, Zem's defiant, westernized, football-playing sister. She also had a leading role in the TV films *Harkis* (Alain Tasma, 2006), alongside Smaïn, *Pour l'amour de Dieu* (Zakia Tahiri and Ahmed Bouchaâla, 2006)[17] and *Le Choix de Myriam* (Malik Chibane,

---

15. Brakni has become known for her strong self-identification as a feminist, her support for the campaign to get women to check their breasts for cancer, and her identification with the Left. See Rachida Brakni (2013), 'Propos recueillis par Mérième Alaoui le lundi 10 juin', < http://www.salamnews.fr/Rachida-Brakni-Enfant-de-la-Republique-je-n-ai-pas-oublie-d-ou-je-viens-et-qui-je-suis_a354.html> [accessed 25 May 2015].

16. See Higbee, *Post-Beur Cinema*, pp. 118–19.

17. In *Pour l'amour de Dieu*, Bekhti plays a schoolgirl who decides to wear the veil, then changes her mind.

2009), as well as co-starring with Gérard Jugnot in *Ali Baba et les 40 voleurs* (Pierre Aknine, 2007). Her first leading role in the cinema was in Nora Hamdi's *Des poupées et des anges* (2008), a low budget first film with a very limited distribution, based on Hamdi's bestselling novel exploring the troubled lives of two Maghrebi-French sisters from the *banlieue*, co-starring Samy Naceri as their abusive but damaged father. However, her breakthrough into popular cinema came thanks to minor roles in two hugely successful thrillers, *Mesrine: L'Instinct de mort* (Jean-François Richet, 2008) and *Un prophète* (Jacques Audiard, 2009), winner of the Jury's Grand Prix at Cannes, where she was the only female actor from the film to mount the red carpet, and went on to marry the lead actor, Tahar Rahim, in 2010.

All That Glitters is another genre film, this time a mainstream comedy clearly directed at a young, popular audience, starring Bekhti as Lila, an attractive, lively young woman of Maghrebi heritage living in Puteaux, alongside director Nakache, herself of Algerian Jewish descent, as her Jewish friend Ely. The film centres on the ups and downs of the friendship between the two young working-class women, both of whom live at home and have boring jobs in Puteaux, and long for a more glamorous life in central Paris. For a time it seems that Lila's unscrupulous attempts to better herself, her lies about where she lives, and her affair with a wealthy young white Frenchman, will come between them; but eventually, when her boyfriend goes back to his former (white) girlfriend, she comes to appreciate the value of her *banlieue* friends, and the film ends joyfully with the renewal of her sparky relationship with Ely.[18] Unlike Bekhti's earlier TV roles where her Maghrebi heritage is often heavily marked, as Lila she plays a thoroughly westernized young woman who is well integrated into a multicultural, consumerist French society. Although troubled by her father's absence – he has made a new home back in Morocco, leaving her unhappy Maghrebi mother still longing for his return – ultimately for Lila, questions of ethnic difference and identity are less important that the acquisition of designer shoes. The film thus showcases Bekhti's appeal both as a comic actor and as the subject of cross-cultural friendship and romance.

In all three of these award-winning roles, the young actors incarnate attractive, feisty, independent-minded young women of Maghrebi origin who are the subjects and agents of their own narratives. As active, geographically mobile, autonomous individuals, they occupy a range of cinematic spaces and resist being defined or limited by their sexuality or, indeed, their ethnic difference. However,

---

18. For a more detailed analysis of *All That Glitters*, see Carrie Tarr, 'From Riots to Designer Shoes: *Tout ce qui brille/All That Glitters* (2010) and Changing Representations of the Banlieue in French Cinema', in *New Suburban Stories*, ed. by Martin Dines and Timotheus Vermeulen (London and New York: Bloomsbury, 2013), pp. 31–9.

the implications of their integration into French society differ from film to film (though it is notable that in no case is the young woman of Maghrebi heritage represented as a practising Muslim). Noémie/Malika/Brakni's struggle for independence in *Chaos* is achieved only through the decisive rejection of her abusive immigrant Maghrebi father and stepfamily (and by extension the patriarchal culture which drove her mother to commit suicide), leading her to choose instead to throw in her lot with two middle class, differently exploited white French women. In contrast, Rym/Herzi in *Couscous* is able to act independently while remaining firmly embedded within her immediate immigrant family environment, sympathetically represented by the small hotel run by her hardworking mother, with its resident group of elderly Maghrebi migrant musicians, and by Slimane's first wife and multi-ethnic extended family. However Lila/Bekhti in *All That Glitters* exemplifies a more consensual, middle road that neither rejects nor fully embraces her Maghrebi heritage. Though she is denied a positive relationship with her father – rather than exploiting her, he has simply abandoned her – she does end up reconciled with her grieving mother, herself a devotee of western-style karaoke. However, her sense of self is ultimately derived from her friendship with Ely and her peers, not to mention her new job at a designer shoe shop in Paris, thereby suggesting that ethnic difference in contemporary (Parisian and *banlieue*) French society might nowadays be of relatively little consequence.

Follow-up films: the Maghreb connection

It is interesting to note that each of these three actors followed their success in France with a leading role in one or more films set in North Africa, roles which tend to underline the specificity of their cultural heritage and ethnic difference rather than emphasizing their hybrid identities and integration into French society. Brakni consolidated her image as a strong, independent woman of Maghrebi origin in two films by Maghrebi women directors. Yasmine Kassari's *L'Enfant endormi* (2005), a Belgian-Moroccan co-production, explores the situation of women affected by the departure of their menfolk seeking work in Europe through the myth that woman are able to control the duration of their pregnancy and the birth of their child during the men's absence. As Halima (a role for which she had to learn Arabic), Brakni plays the rebellious cousin of a newly married wife who, as the myth has it, seemingly puts the birth of her child on hold, until she realizes she is unlikely to see her husband again. Then in Djamila Sahraoui's feminist road movie *Barakat!/Ça suffit!*, a Franco-Tunisian co-production (2006), she has an even tougher role as Amel, a doctor, whose journalist husband goes missing during the Algerian civil war in the 1990s, and who attempts, with a woman friend, a former resistance fighter, to find him, a quest which demonstrates more generally the oppression and exploitation of women during Algeria's *années de plomb*.

Herzi also followed her success in France with two films by women of Maghrebi origin. In Souad El-Bouhati's *Française* (2008) she plays Sofia, a troubled, rebellious adolescent born in France, who as a child identifies completely with her French experience and suffers from her family's decision to return to the Maghreb. In *Les Secrets* (2010), Raja Amari's follow-up to *Satin rouge* (2002), she plays Aïcha, another troubled adolescent, the daughter of a woman living secretly in the underground servants' quarters of a deserted villa, who discovers, when the owners' grandson returns for a summer holiday with his wife, that her elder sister is her real mother, having been raped by the villa's owner. While *Française* plays on Herzi's feisty image as a French-born young woman of Maghrebi origin, her role in *Les Secrets* introduces a more ambiguous, unstable, threatening element as the women exact their revenge.

None of these four films was as successful in France as the first film made in the Maghreb by Leïla Bekhti following her success in *All That Glitters,* namely Radu Mihaileanu's comedy, *La Source des femmes* (2011; 757,797 spectators in France), a group film which also starred Herzi, Sabrina Ouazani,[19] Palestinian actor Hiam Abbas and Algerian star Biyouna. A Jewish filmmaker of Romanian origin, Mihaileaunu had already enjoyed popular success exploring different communities with *Train de vie* (1998), *Va, vis et deviens* (2005) and *Le Concert* (2009). Set in an anonymous Maghrebi village, *La Source* centres on the village women's revolt against their menfolk who spend their days in the café and refuse to help their wives carry water on the arduous journey from the well, even when it causes a pregnant woman to lose her child. Bekhti has the central role of Leïla, an intelligent young woman who, supported by her enlightened schoolteacher husband, persuades the other women to go on a sex strike, a role which earned her a nomination for Best Female Actor at the 2012 Césars. Herzi meanwhile plays Loubna, a naïve, illiterate younger woman who refuses the idea of an arranged marriage, and decides to leave the village alone when she discovers Leïla has been writing the letters she thought were from an admirer. *La Source* draws on a gallery of rather tired comic stereotypes, both male and female, in order to critique Arab/Berber women's condition in the Maghreb, a theme which continues to appeal to a mainstream French audience.

Follow-up films set in metropolitan France

Thus Brakni, Herzi and Bekhti have all three enjoyed ethnically marked leading roles as independent-minded young Maghrebi women in films set in the Maghreb. However, apart from *La Source*, these films have only achieved modest returns at the box office and have not generally contributed to their star status in the French film industry. The rest of this article examines each actor's career path in

---

19. Sabrina Ouazani was the co-star of Abdellatif Kechiche's award-winning *L'Esquive* (2004).

metropolitan France, assessing the range of roles they have been able to play, the extent to which they have remained the subjects of their own narratives rather than being objectified and contained, and the degree to which their roles are ethnically marked or promote a more fluid, non-specific ethnic identity. In the process it raises the question as to whether the ability to inhabit unmarked roles is a sign of the integration of ethnic others into contemporary notions of Frenchness, or of the erasure of ethnic and cultural difference.

Rachida Brakni

Rachida Brakni began with ethnically marked minor roles in *Loin* (André Téchiné, 2001) and *Comme un avion* (Marie-France Pisier, 2002), followed by a non-Maghrebi co-starring role in *L'Outremangeur* (Thierry Binisti, 2003), playing opposite Eric Cantona, her future husband, as Elsa, a presumed murderess, who bargains for her freedom by agreeing to witness the eponymous obese detective eating his evening meal each night. She had minor non-Arab roles in two genre films: as a Jewish woman in the comedy *Ne quittez pas!* (Arthur Joffé, 2004), and as Sylvie, an incorruptible French police officer in the skateboard thriller *Skate or Die* (Miguel Courtois, 2008), followed by an ethnically marked supporting role as Leïla in spy thriller *Secret Défense* (Philippe Haïm, 2008). In *La Ligne droite* (Régis Wargnier, 2011) she co-stars as Leïla again, this time a disgraced runner, a former prisoner, who helps a blind (male) athlete perform competitively.

She has also branched out in two films by (and starring) porn director HPG, as Rachida in *On ne devrait pas exister* (2006) and, with her husband, as Marion in *Les Mouvements du bassin* (2012), and as Claire in another film with Cantona which explores deviant sexuality, *La Part animale* (Sébastien Jaudeau, 2007). While these roles show her independence as an actor, willing to undertake daring roles and flout expectations of modesty (she also plays Claude, a lesbian antiques dealer in Alain Tasma's TV drama, *La Surprise* (2007), co-starring Mireille Perrier), the films have not attracted large audiences.

However, the most successful film she has been in since *Chaos* is the hit comedy *Neuilly sa mère!* (Gabriel Laferrière, 2009; 2,452,007 spectators in France), in which she plays Djemila de Chazelle, a former barrister of Maghrebi origin, now the wife of an aristocratic white businessman living in Neuilly. Disappointingly, her role functions as the necessary if implausible starting point for a comedy of ethnic integration centring on Sami, her young nephew from a working-class housing estate in Chalon-sur-Saône, and his relationship with, among others, her pompous white stepson Charles, rather than providing her with a comic starring vehicle in her own right. Furthermore, in the crime drama *Une affaire d'état* (Eric Valette, 2009), despite a seemingly central role as Nora Chahyd, an intense, enterprising detective of Maghrebi origin, she is marginalized within a narrative which privileges the points of view of her white male co-stars.

In the more recent TV political thriller *Silences d'État* (Frédéric Berthe, 2013), she has a similar role as white French spin doctor Claire Ferran, who manages, with the help of a journalist, to uncover a sinister political plot.

Most of Brakni's films after *Chaos* set in France have been made by male directors, and have alternated between ethnically marked and unmarked roles, though the ethnically marked roles have not generally involved placing the character within the wider construction of the Maghrebi community, except in the case of *Neuilly sa mère!* The two films she has made with women directors are Claire Simon's *Les Bureaux de Dieu* (2008), a star-studded, multi-ethnic group film in which she plays Yasmina, a counsellor of Maghrebi origin giving advice on contraception and abortion, and Françoise Charpiat's first film, *Cheba Louisa* (2013), Brakni's latest film at the time of writing, a comedy of ethnic integration and cross-cultural female friendship in which, recalling *Chaos*, she plays once more opposite a white female French star, this time Isabelle Carré (who also co-starred in *Les Bureaux de Dieu*). *Cheba Louisa,* co-written with Mariem Hamidat, centres on the conflict of identity facing a second generation woman of Maghrebi heritage in contemporary France, addressing the same, now rather clichéd, problematic as Yamina Benguigui's popular *Aïcha* series on French television.[20] As Djemila, Brakni plays a successful young lawyer leading an impossible double life: in the insurance company where she works, she is the perfect professional who is also enjoying a love affair with a white colleague; in the *banlieue*, her mother (Biyouna) expects her to abide by traditional Maghrebi values and accept the Maghrebi-French fiancé she has arranged for her. The film opens with Djemila moving in to her own flat, determined to enjoy her independence, where her life becomes entangled with that of Emma (Carré), a kooky young single mother living on the same landing, whose musician partner has died and who has problems making ends meet. Having a home of her own also enables Djemila to indulge her love of Algerian chaâba music, thanks to the memorabilia relating to her late grandmother, Cheba Louisa, a former singing star, secretly entrusted to her by her affectionate father (her stern but loving mother cannot bear to hear talk of her). A key scene shows Djemila singing along to the projection of her grandmother's performance, both being played and voiced by Brakni. And her singing, accompanied by Emma on the darbuka, eventually enables her not only to pay off Emma's debt but also to assume a Maghrebi heritage that has a place for independent women and women's music, and gives her the strength to dismiss the two men in her life. The move matches Brakni's own move towards a parallel singing career.

---

20. *Aïcha* (2009), *Aïcha, job à tout prix* (2011), *Aïcha, la grande débrouille* (2011) and *Aïcha, vacances infernales* (2013).

Hafsia Herzi

It is noticeable that, after *Couscous,* Herzi's first starring roles set in France require her to represent a more naïve, often heavily sexualized and/or subordinate young woman. Alternating ethnically marked and unmarked roles, these films tend to tame her sexuality and mute her desire for independence by matching her with a series of often inappropriate (white) male co-stars who constitute the primary focus of the narrative. In Alain Guiraudie's comedy, *Le Roi de l'évasion* (2009), she plays Curly, a young, sexy, non-Maghrebi-French schoolgirl, who seeks to escape an exploitative family situation by seducing Armand (Ludovic Berthillot), an overweight, anxious, gay, agricultural salesman, after he saves her from being mugged.[21] In Francis Huster's *Un homme et son chien* (2009), a star vehicle for an ageing Jean-Paul Belmondo, she plays Leïla, a young maid who takes pity on the old man as he gets rejected by her employer, his former mistress, and becomes increasingly destitute; in Xavier de Choudens' crime drama, *Joseph et la fille* (2010), starring an ageing Jacques Dutronc, she plays Julie, a young *banlieue* woman, who falls in love with the eponymous Joseph, her dead father's best friend, when he undertakes to rob a casino with her. And in Teddy Lussi-Modeste's *Jimmy Rivière* (2011), set in a Gypsy community near Grenoble, she has a supporting role as Sonia, the former girlfriend of the eponymous, conflicted Jimmy (Guillaume Gouix). Like Brakni, Herzi appears to be alternating ethnically marked and unmarked roles, but her ethnically marked roles do not locate her in relation to the wider Maghrebi-French community.

The inability of film-makers in metropolitan France to cast Herzi in a key, complex starring role is also evident in the other films she has made. In *Ma compagne de nuit* (Isabelle Brocard, 2011), her role as Marine, a hospital linen maid who volunteers to look after Julie, a terminal cancer patient, is secondary to that of her co-star Emmanuelle Béart. In *L'Apollonide: souvenirs de maison close* (Bertrand Bonello, 2011), despite a prominent place in the film's credits, her role as Samira, an Algerian prostitute, is not explored in any detail. In *Elle s'en va* (Emmanuelle Bercot, 2013), a road movie and star vehicle for Catherine Deneuve, her unmarked role as Jeanne, a waitress in Deneuve's restaurant, is a very minor one, even if she is accepted as a member of Deneuve's extended screen family. In fact her most successful film after *Couscous* and *La Source* is *Le Chat du rabbin* (Joann Sfar, 2011; 514,960 spectators in France), an animated feature in which she voices the rabbi's daughter. Her latest film at the time of writing, however, is *La Marche* (Nabil Ben Yadir, 2013), a Franco-Belgian group film which relocates her within the Maghrebi community in France.

---

21. Herzi commented that she wanted 'de pouvoir parler arabe dans un film, et jouer Charlotte dans un autre'. See Hafsia Herzi and Sandrine Bonnaire, *L'Espoir est féminin: Hafsia Herzi, rencontre avec Sandrine Bonnaire* (Montreuil: Éditions de l'œil, 2009), p. 26.

A fictionalized reconstruction of the 1983 *Marche pour l'égalité et contre le racisme*, the film centres on an initially small group of protesters from Les Minguettes in Lyon, led by Mohamed (Tewfik Jallab) and the priest Christian Dubois (Olivier Gourmet), who are joined among others by Kheira (Lubna Azabal), Mohamed's fierce, intellectual aunt, and her student niece Monia, played by Herzi. Initially quiet and subdued, Monia begins an affair with Sylvain, a young white French marcher, before being raped and branded by men from the Front National, an event which enables her to find a voice and express her defiance, refusing to be a victim. But it is television that Herzi has to thank for a more substantial historical starring role, namely as the eponymous Djamila Boupacha in Caroline Huppert's *Pour Djamila* (2012), co-starring Marina Hands as lawyer Gisèle Halimi.

Given the limited nature of the film roles she has been given in France, it is perhaps not surprising to find that Herzi, more than the other two actors discussed here, has turned to films by overseas directors, not just in the Maghreb. In 2008 she starred in the award-winning *L'Aube du monde* (Abbas Fahdel), a film set in Iraq, where she plays Zahra, the widow of an Iraqi soldier. And in the last three years she has made four films with non-French directors, three of them women. She plays Sarah, a young woman of Moroccan parentage, reprising the theme of *Française*, in *Le Sac de farine* (2012) by Moroccan-Belgian actor/director Kadija Leclere, Palestinian Hajar in *Héritage* (2012) directed by Hiam Abbass (with whom she co-starred in *Les Secrets* and *La Source*), Moroccan Karima in *Exit Marrakech* (2014) by German director Caroline Link, and Hafsia, a Tunisian migrant seeking an abortion in Sicily, in *War Story* (2014) by American director Mark Jackson (in which she co-stars with Catherine Keener and Ben Kingsley). However, though such roles might signal Herzi's potential for international stardom, only *Exit Marrakech* achieved a sizeable audience in France.

She will next appear in the latest film by Algerian émigré director Mahmoud Zemmouri, *Certifié Halal*, not yet released in France, which, as a comedy about arranged marriages, may enable her to regain a French audience. So far, however, none of her screen roles has matched the power and intensity of her role in *Couscous*.

Leïla Bekhti

Before her success in *All That Glitters*, Bekhti had shown herself well able to perform in both genre films and social realist films exploring the conflicts facing the daughters of immigrants in postcolonial France. She has subsequently appeared in a number of other French comedies of ethnic integration. After a small supporting role in Anne Depetrini's cross-cultural romantic comedy *Il reste du jambon?* (2010), starring Ramzy Bedia, she enjoyed a leading role in Audrey Estraougou's *Toi, moi, les autres* (2011), a musical comedy with a political edge (including a montage of documentary footage showing support for the sans-papiers of Saint Bernard), in which Bekhti, along with the rest of the cast, is encouraged to display her singing and dancing talents. Instead of the miserabilist approach to the Maghrebi immigrant family of the earlier *Des poupées et des anges*, *Toi, moi, les autres* combines a focus on the colourful residents of a multi-ethnic district of Paris with a cross-cultural romance in which motherless law student Leïla (Bekhti) is eventually won over by Gabriel (Benjamin Siksou), the indolent son of a wealthy police commissioner, who uses his position to prevent the deportation of Tina, Leïla's black hairdresser friend and surrogate mother, and so allow a happy ending. Bekhti also co-stars in Géraldine Nakache's rather banal follow-up to *All That Glitters*, the group film *Nous York* (2012), where she plays Samia, Sienna Miller's assistant in New York, alongside Nakache as Gabrielle, who works in an old people's home, and a trio of young men from the *banlieue* who visit to celebrate Samia's thirtieth birthday. And in *Itinéraire bis* (2011), a romantic comedy directed by Jean-Luc Perréard, she has a leading role as the glamorous Leïla who loses one (white) boyfriend, but eventually gains another.

She has also had starring roles in a number of white male-authored films which are not comedies. In Cédric Kahn's social realist drama *Une vie meilleure* (2012) she plays Nadia, a waitress with a young child, Slimane, who dreams of opening a restaurant with her new white boyfriend Yann (Guillaume Canet). When they can no longer make ends meet, however, she leaves for Canada, leaving Yann to look after Slimane, only to find herself in prison when Yann and Slimane try to find her. In police thriller *Mains armées* (Pierre Jolivet, 2012), she plays Maya Dervin, a cop, the daughter of another cop, Lucas Skali, played by Roschdy Zem, who had abandoned her at birth, and with whom she finds herself working in the course of a complicated drugs and arms trafficking case. In the psychological thriller *Avant l'hiver* (Philippe Claudel, 2013), she plays a psychotic young woman, Lou, real name Sabiah, a student of Maghrebi origin who haunts a surgeon played by Daniel Auteuil in a role which recalls the latter's haunting in Michel Haneke's *Caché*; ultimately she kills herself knowing he will find her body, and leaves him a tape of her grandmother teaching her to sing, a song sung by Bekhti herself. In her latest film, *Maintenant ou jamais* (Serge Frydman, 2014), another crime drama, she has an ethnically unmarked role as Juliette, a dutiful wife and mother and part-time piano teacher, who in protest at the redundancy of her husband, Charlie, which puts an end to her dream of life in an architect-designed house, organizes a robbery of the bank where he worked, assisted by Manu (Nicholas Devauchelle), a man who had earlier tried to mug her, and whom she comes to care for. However, neither this film nor the others she has appeared in since *All That Glitters*, have approached the same level of box office success.

Her latest film project, however, is the role of Albertine in *L'Astragale* by female actor/director Brigitte Sy (2015), based on Albertine Sarrazin's eponymous semi-autobiographical novel recounting her escape from prison and love affair with Julien, a small-time criminal played by Reda Kateb (the Gypsy in *Un prophète*). Thus whereas Brakni and Herzi appear to be consolidating their careers with parts which return them to their ethnic origins and community roots, Bekhti seems to be moving towards more ethnically non-specific roles, an indication that her star image has become 'detachable' from her Maghrebi heritage.[22]

Conclusion

So what do the acting profiles of these actors tell us about the integration of young French women of Maghrebi heritage into the French film industry and hence the consciousness of mainstream French audiences? Clearly, their star image is also mediated by the popular press and complicated by actions and decisions which are beyond the scope of this article. This is particularly true of Brakni and Bekhti, who are both currently part of a celebrity couple, which in Brakni's case has led to her posing with husband Cantona for fashion house Kooples in 2012/13. Both have also been models for L'Oréal, Brakni in 2008, Bekhti since 2011, thus promoting a multiethnic image of French glamour. And Brakni is notable, too, for developing other strings to her bow, as a recording artist (she has a second album due, mostly in Arabic), and as a director (she is currently preparing her first feature film, *De sas en sas*, a prison drama).[23]

In terms of their screen roles, however, all three have to date maintained solid records of employment, to a noticeably greater extent than promising young leading actors of earlier films foregrounding young women of Maghrebi origin.[24] Furthermore, their screen presence has been welcomed both in films where they directly represent their ethnic origins (as long as they are not represented as practising Muslims),[25] and in films where they assume Franco-French names and status, an indication that their ethnic difference may be increasingly irrelevant in mainstream representations of Frenchness. Their acceptance as part of the wider French showbiz family is also indicated by the fact that all three have co-starred with major Franco-French screen stars, both male and female. And all three have

---

22. The term is used in the analysis of Sami Bouajila's star image in Murray Pratt and Denis Provencher, '(Re)casting Sami Bouajila: An Ambiguous Model of Integration, Belonging and Citizenship', in Durmelat and Swamy (eds.), *Screening Integration,* pp. 194–210.

23. Herzi, too, is currently preparing to direct her first feature film, a prison drama inspired by her mother entitled *Bonne mère*, set in Marseille and produced by Abdellatif Kechiche.

24. For example, Nora in *Les Histoires d'amour finissent mal en général* (Anne Fontaine, 1993) or Seloua Hamse in *Douce France* (Malik Chibane, 1995).

25. Herzi has recently starred in the César-nominated short film, *Où je mets ma pudeur* (Sébastien Bailly, 2013), playing a Muslim art history student expected to remove her veil in order to comment on Ingres's *La Grande Odalisque*.

appeared in both genre and auteur films and in a range of roles which transcend stereotypes, particularly in the case of Brakni who is repeatedly cast in high-powered, physically demanding, professional roles, including roles which show her on both sides of the law.

If these factors are indicative of their integration into mainstream French cinema, it is also the case that relatively few of the metropolitan films starring Brakni and Herzi have directly addressed their status in relation to the wider Maghrebi community, the exceptions being Brakni's secondary role in *Neuilly sa mère!* and her co-starring role in the more recent *Cheba Louisa* and Herzi's secondary role in *La Marche* and co-starring role in the forthcoming *Certifié Halal*. Furthermore, Herzi in particular has suffered from being cast in a number of subordinate roles in relation to her Franco-French co-stars, be it as maid, waitress, delinquent or prostitute, and/or in roles which risk confining her to the 'sexy beurette' stereotype, no doubt a reason for her seeking job satisfaction in films made outside France. In contrast, Bekhti had built her career on a string of ethnically marked roles as a feisty young woman of Maghrebi origin before her award-winning role in *All That Glitters*, and has continued to appear in a series of comedies of ethnic integration, notably *Toi, moi, les autres*. However, her more recent roles show a move towards ethnically blind casting in crime dramas that challenge her drive towards independence, as in the forthcoming *L'Astragale*, which, like the earlier *Mains armées* co-starring Bekhti with Roschdy Zem, showcases two stars of Maghrebi origin (Bekhti with Reda Kateb) in unmarked roles. Hopefully this will not preclude her taking on more ethnically marked roles in the future, since it is the ability to move between different types of roles that best indicates the French film industry's acceptance of ethnic and cultural difference as integral components of contemporary Frenchness. In the case of all three actors, however, their follow-up films (apart from *Neuilly sa mère!*) have to date failed to bring them the same degree of success and/or recognition as their César award-wining films, and their achievements are as yet not comparable with that of their male peers.

Nottingham French Studies 54.3 (2015): 312–327
DOI: 10.3366/nfs.2015.0129

WHAT'S 'FRENCH' ABOUT FRENCH STUDIES?

CHARLES FORSDICK

In Memoriam: Amy Wygant, 1953–2012

If we could today – without the burden or benefit of precedent, tradition, or institutional inertia – invent a field called 'French and Francophone Studies', what would it look like? What would be its purpose, not only within our university institutions but also the broader sphere of political and cultural debate and production? Upon what definitions of the terms 'French' or 'Francophone' would it be founded? What would be its horizon, its sense of its own future? How would we justify its existence to those whom we would ask to support it – financially, morally, and institutionally – as well as to those whom we hope will comprise its constituency?[1]

Those reflecting on what is 'French' about 'French studies' in the early twenty-first century are obliged to consider the transformations evident in increasingly pluralized or diversified objects of study, as well as the radical changes in the ways in which those objects are now approached. At the same time, such a reflection still necessitates urgent exploration of the semantic gap between what – in Mary Gallagher's terms – is to be understood by 'France' and what is meant by 'French'.[2] Picking up already on this gap in a 1991 intervention on 'the scope and methodology of French', Christophe Campos described the ways in which 'French is unusual, but not quite unique, amongst university subjects in choosing to designate itself by an adjective instead of a noun'. He continued:

We talk of History and not historical, and Chemistry and not chemical, Physics and not physical. But in our subject we have for about 120 years now mostly been content with the adjective French. Now as describers of linguistic systems, we know that adjectives can serve as nouns; but they're not very good denotative nouns

---

1. Laurent Dubois and Achille Mbembe, 'Nous sommes tous francophones', *French Politics, Culture and Society*, 32:2 (2014), 40–8 (p. 40).

2. On this subject, see Mary Gallagher, 'Revisiting the "Others' Others", or the Bankruptcy of Otherness as a Value in Literature in French', *Women's Studies Review*, 6 (1999), 51–9 (p. 51), cited by Roger Little, 'World Literature in French; or Is Francophonie Frankly Phoney?', *European Review*, 9:4 (2001), 421–36 (p. 425).

because they have an arbitrary field of reference. They are extendable in the user's mind ('of or pertaining to' in dictionary language) and they have an unpredictable denotation when they are substantivised.[3]

Almost twenty-five years later, it is fruitful to revisit Campos's provocative reflection on the 'scope and methodology of French', not least because – as he implied it would, although perhaps not in ways imaginable then – this unpredictability of denotation has permitted the rapid expansion of French studies beyond its initial gallocentric, Hexagonal and primarily literary focus into the multifaceted and geographically variegated set of practices it seeks to encompass today.[4] In asking, in 2015, 'what's "French" about French studies?', there is a need to reflect on a new range of variables; part of the task is also to question whether a focus on the extent to which disciplinary practices are 'still French' obscures the more telling issue as to whether they were 'ever French', that is, whether the signifier of the epithet 'French' was ever stable, coherent and conducive to any form of disciplinary consensus.[5] Some of the variables to which 'French' now refers relate to our objects of study (and most notably the changing nature and status of France and the wider Francosphere, subject in particular to processes of Europeanization and globalization).[6] Other new aspects are linked to recent and emerging practices in Arts and Humanities research by which those objects are studied (most notably postcolonialism, but also new forms of comparative, transnational and global analysis). At the same

3.   Christophe Campos, 'The Scope and Methodology of French', in *French in the 90s: A Transbinary Conference July 1991*, ed. by Jennifer Birkett and Michael Kelly (Birmingham: Birmingham Modern Languages Publications, 1992), pp. 33–8 (p. 33).

4.   For a reflection on the parallel shifts in French studies in the U.S.A. during the same period, see Arthur Goldhammer, 'A Few Thoughts on the Future of French Studies', *French Politics, Culture and Society*, 32:2 (2014), 15–20.

5.   Janell Watson notes: 'French was perhaps never a stable entity, even before the coming into being of *la Francophonie* and even in a decidedly national context, as Anderson suggests in describing the nation as an imagined community.' See 'Culture and the Future of French Studies', *Contemporary French and Francophone Studies*, 14:5 (2010), 477–84 (p. 480).

6.   For a discussion of the impact of Europeanization and globalization, see George Ross, 'Can French Studies Exist Today?', *French Politics, Culture and Society*, 32:2 (2014), 9–14. It is important to note that there is evidence of a similar diversification and even 'becoming-transnational' among researchers in, for example, German and Italian. The AHRC is currently funding a major project on 'Transnationalizing Modern Languages: Mobility, Identity and Translation in Modern Italian Cultures', of which details are available here: < http://www.transnationalmodernlanguages.ac.uk/> [accessed 31 March 2015], and there is a parallel interest in 'German in the World', to which a conference was devoted at the Institute of Modern Languages Research in June 2014 (see < http://events.sas.ac.uk/imlr/events/view/15745/German + in + the + World> [accessed 31 March 2015]).

time, there is a need to acknowledge the implications of advocacy for a post-disciplinary university, a vision set out by scholars such as Mark Taylor in his 2009 *New York Times* op-ed piece on 'the end of the university as we know it': Taylor's call to 'abolish permanent departments, even for undergraduate education, and create problem-focused programs' raises key questions for languages, which in such models risk being reduced to linguistic competence rather than complex disciplinary skills sets.[7] And finally there is a range of institutional or disciplinary considerations relating to such cross-disciplinary working and, more particularly, to the recognition that French studies is a sub-disciplinary field to be located in relation to a wider disciplinary area of Modern Languages.

To begin to answer the question: 'what *is* "French" about French studies?' requires engagement, then, with the question: 'what *was* "French" about French studies?' As Amy Wygant noted in a short article on the 1918 report prepared by Sir Stanley Leathes on 'Modern Studies' (the outcome of what remains one of the most serious official enquiries conducted into the place of languages in UK education), those who work in French have not shown the same interest as their colleagues in, for instance, Classics or English, in their disciplinary origins and heritage.[8] The objective of such an exploration of (sub)disciplinary genealogies and change is not that of mourning what has been lost, but instead of reflecting on what might be retained as the field continues to evolve and to address a variety of current challenges.[9] As Malcolm Bowie noted in his 1992 sketch of French studies in the UK: 'pour préparer aux batailles qui nous attendent, nous ne pouvions faire mieux que revenir un moment, sans complaisance, sur le passé des

---

7. Mark C. Taylor, 'End the University as We Know It', *New York Times*, 26 April 2009. It is striking that for Taylor, 'language' is one of the 'broad range of topics around which such zones of inquiry could be organized'.

8. Amy Wygant, 'Modern Studies: Historiography and Directions', *French Studies Bulletin*, 30 (2009), 75–8 (p. 75). For the Leathes report, see *Modern Studies: Being the Report of the Committee on the Position of Modern Languages in the Education System of Great Britain* (London: HMSO, 1918). A useful analysis of its place in the history of Modern Languages is provided by Susan Bayley, 'Modern Languages: An "Ideal of Humane Learning": The Leathes Report of 1918', *Journal of Educational Administration and History*, 23:2 (1991), 11–24. On the emergence of French studies within the frame of Modern Languages during this period, see also Susan Bayley, 'Modern Languages as Emerging Curricular Subjects in England 1864–1914', *History of Education Society Bulletin*, 47 (1991), 23–31, and G.T. Clapton and W. Stewart, *Les Études françaises dans l'enseignement en Grande-Bretagne* (Paris: Les Belles Lettres, 1929).

9. For an AHRC-funded network exploring the history of teaching and learning Modern Languages in the UK, see < http://historyofmfl.weebly.com > [accessed 31 March 2015]. Members of the network contributed to a recent special issue of *Language and History* (57:1 (2014)) on 'Building the History of Language Learning and Teaching (HoLLT)', ed. by Nicola McLelland and Richard Smith.

études françaises à l'université et sur leurs réalisations les plus considérables.'[10]
In one of the few histories of French studies in the UK, Christophe Campos
tracked the evolution of the field from these origins in some detail. In an article
written in 1989, a decade into Margaret Thatcher's government and as the French
subject community was suffering from what he calls 'une cure d'amaigrissement',
Campos reflected on the emergence of his subject area:

> Dès l'instant où une nation existe au point de chercher à se connaître, sa prise de
> conscience passe par une comparaison entre sa propre culture et celles d'autres
> nations: les peuples, comme les individus, ne se connaissent pleinement qu'à travers
> l'image et le regard de l'autre. [...] C'est la France, tour à tour royaume jumeau et
> meilleur ennemi, à la fois partenaire et rival parmi les civilisations de l'ancien
> monde, qui est pour le Britannique le premier pas vers l'étranger, donc vers
> lui-même. Des contrastes multiples entre les deux pays – linguistiques, religieux,
> politiques – ont constamment maintenu l'intérêt de la comparaison. La géographie
> de la Manche y est sans doute aussi pour beaucoup: tant pour les enfants des nobles
> effectuant leur 'grand tour' que pour les petits bataillons de consommateurs qui
> prennent d'assaut les bacs pour les 'mini-tours', 'the Continent begins at Calais.'[11]

French was present on university curricula from the eighteenth century, but
as a supplementary activity and restricted to language acquisition alone.[12] From
the 1870s, however, under the influence of philology (and the key ideas that
belles lettres were an eminently exportable reflection of the core of a foreign
civilization), a recognizably modern sub-discipline began to emerge in the ancient
and 'red brick' universities. As Wygant notes, exploration of these origins has
much to teach us – especially in the crucial period immediately following World
War 1, about 'developing attitudes towards neighbourliness, foreignness, gender,
conflict and space'.[13] French was, as Susan Bayley explains cogently, in the
vanguard of a post-war reaction against 'an antiquated educational system which
overemphasized Classics at the expense of modern languages and science',[14] and
the committee investigating this situation, chaired by Leathes, advocated the
integration of a range of living languages (and the cultures they represented)
on the grounds of utility, but remained committed to an assumed primacy of

10. Malcolm Bowie, 'Les Études françaises dans les universités britanniques: une esquisse',
    Littérature, 87 (1992), 77–87 (p. 87).
11. Christophe Campos, 'L'Enseignement du français dans les universités britanniques',
    Franco-British Studies, 8 (1989), 69–108 (pp. 69–70).
12. On this early history, see Kathleen Lambley, *The Teaching and Cultivation of the French
    Language in England during Tudor and Stuart Times* (Manchester: Manchester
    University Press, 1920), and Michèle Cohen, *Fashioning Masculinity: National Identity
    and Language in the Eighteenth Century* (London: Routledge, 1996).
13. Wygant, 'Modern Studies', p. 75.
14. Bayley, 'Modern Languages: An "Ideal of Humane Learning"', p. 11.

French in schools and universities. Key to Leathes's recommendations was a proposed anglicization of the professoriate (a move less popular among teachers of French than those of other languages), and this was a direction taken in the interwar period as an indigenously 'British' French studies attempted to emerge. Leathes had articulated a clear vision of what he dubbed 'Modern Studies', seen as an 'ideal of humane learning':

> The Universities should train up for the service of the nation an abundant supply of men and women capable of acquiring, digesting, arranging and imparting the vast amount of knowledge concerning foreign countries which can only be obtained by study, and travel, and personal intercourse. This knowledge comprises not only philology and imaginative literature, which have held too exclusive a monopoly in the past, but also history, economics, sociology, politics, art, technology and philosophy.[15]

Defining and locating itself in relation to Classics, philology and the persistently influential *lettres modernes*,[16] French did not, however, adopt this expansive, inclusive, even permissive definition, but emphasized instead literary translation and the reading in historical context of canonical French literary texts. The interwar study of French was part of a turn away from the Classics, not so much in terms of rejecting previous paradigms but of supplanting them, a manœuvre evident in the title of John Orr's inaugural lecture in Edinburgh in 1933, 'French, the Third Classic', which neatly encapsulates the persistence of study of a *national* culture through its literature whilst unwittingly including an indication of the field's inbuilt obsolescence. For Orr, the rationale for studying French was fundamentally a contrastive one: 'while preserving the spontaneity of the British genius', he wrote, the aim of the study of French literature was 'to temper it, to enhance it with that sense of style and disciplined art which a contact with classicism bestows'.[17]

Conflict and its aftermath had a clear impact on the study of French following World War II, when the 'modern' element originally envisaged on Leathes' *Modern Studies* report was once again asserted. A National Union of Students anti-philological protest was published in 1946 in *Universities Quarterly* – almost certainly motivated by recently demobbed students who saw a radical mismatch between their recent experience of French, France and the French, and

---

15. *Modern Studies*, pp. 54–5.
16. For a discussion of the ways in which Modern Languages is one of a number of modern disciplinary fields to emerge from philology, see James Turner, *Philology: The Forgotten Origins of the Modern Humanities* (Princeton and Oxford: Princeton University Press, 2014).
17. John Orr, *French the Third Classic: An Inaugural Lecture given at the University of Edinburgh on 10th October 1933* (Edinburgh: Oliver and Boyd, 1933), pp. 30–1.

the version of Frenchness being proposed in University curricula –, and this set the tone for self-reflexive debates around disciplinary identity in the post-war period.[18] These debates focussed in particular on the parameters of the field, on methodological approaches and on the importance (for many fundamental) of linguistic competence. They led, in a rapidly expanding Higher Education sector, to the cracking of 'coherence', and resultant 'state of disarray', which Campos identified in the 1960s.[19] In his account of this transitional moment, the establishment of new agendas is seen to be reflected institutionally during the following decade: in the emergence in 1975 of the group of researchers who would subsequently launch *Paragraph* (a response to the *problème de méthode*, and in particular the rejection of engagement with *la nouvelle critique*); the establishment in 1979 of the Association for the Study of Modern and Contemporary France and the launch of the journal *French Cultural Studies* in 1990 (a reflection of the *problème de champ*); and the development in 1981 of the Association for French Language Studies (a reaction to the *problème de compétence*).[20] There was resistance to such moves, epitomized by Lloyd Austin's reported retort at the Society for French Studies conference held in Hull in 1983:

> We have spent a great deal of time building up our subject, we have got it estab-
> lished on a firm basis of literary history, and we're not going to let it be dismantled
> for the sake of contemporary fads.[21]

and even by Campos who, from the perspective of the 1980s, deploying value-laden terminology, articulated a fear of fragmentation and a desire for terminological coherence around the epithet 'French' that returns me to the subject of the current article:

> Il ne nous appartient pas de préjuger de l'avenir, sauf d'espérer qu'une méthode, ou
> à tout le moins un projet d'ensemble se superpose au bric-à-brac actuel et y ramène
> plus de cohérence que n'en garantit l'adjectif 'French'.[22]

---

18. See 'Why Compulsory Philology?', *Universities Quarterly*, 1 (1946–47), 57–69. Cited in Campos, 'L'Enseignement du français dans les universités britanniques', pp. 87–8.

19. Campos, 'The Scope and Methodology of French', p. 36. For an overview of curricula in this period, see *Modern Languages in the Universities: A Guide to Courses of Study in Five European Languages at Universities in the United Kingdom*, ed. by H.H. Stern (London: Macmillan, 1965).

20. See Campos, 'L'Enseignement du français dans les universités britanniques', p. 100.

21. Lloyd Austin, Society for French Studies conference, Hull, 1983. Cited by Campos, 'L'Enseignement du français dans les universités britanniques', p. 94.

22. Campos, 'L'Enseignement du français dans les universités britanniques', p. 107.

Largely unquestioned, however, throughout the twentieth century, up to and including the contributions to the volume on *French in the 90s* cited above, were the geographical – and essentially Hexagonal – boundaries of this 'French' in 'French studies'.[23] The diversification evident in emerging 'fads' was variously advocated, tolerated or denounced, but it occurred within a predominantly French national frame, with occasional extension to European Francophone countries whose literature tends to be granted an honorary French status. A respondent to Colin Evans's questions regarding the 'experience of teaching and learning modern languages in British universities' summarized this approach: 'You can put anything on a French course as long as it has some link with France, is intellectually respectable, and makes the students work'; and this was an observation that Evans himself saw not as a threat but as a strength: 'this multiplicity, while confusing to the university, has actually enabled the discipline to adapt with great rapidity to the changing environment.'[24]

Adaptation to a changing environment, and in particular to the increasingly evident challenges of diversity, has meant that the changes to French studies in the past quarter century – in the period encompassed by the special issue in which this article appears – have arguably been as significant, if not more significant, than those witnessed over the preceding century since the emergence of the field in a recognizably modern form. Even those who adhere to a purely national definition of the 'French' in French studies have been forced to reassess their assumptions. Not only have we witnessed a radical rescaling of the perceived influence of France and its culture, exaggerated but nevertheless encapsulated in volumes providing an external gaze, such as Donald Morrison's *Death of French Culture* (2010), where the waning of French influence is associated with what Oana Panaïté has dubbed 'la précarisation du français au sein de l'institution universitaire';[25] but also, at the same time, we have seen a radical reassessment of the national (in both historical and contemporary frames), as an autonomous unit of analysis, and a parallel redefinition of 'Frenchness' (beyond the monolingual, universalist and ethnically-determined assumptions with which the term was long associated). Morrison's terminology is arguably unhelpful, but in describing the

---

23. In this respect, UK French studies differs from, for instance, French studies in the U.S.A., where pioneers such as the African-American scholar and diplomat Will Mercer Cook had from an early stage advocated for the inclusion of the literary production of other Francophone countries and representations of Black cultures.

24. Colin Evans, *Language People: The Experience of Teaching and Learning Modern Languages in British Universities* (Milton Keynes: Open University Press, 1988), pp. 173, 177.

25. Donald Morrison's *Death of French Culture* (Cambridge: Polity, 2010). This was first published as *Que reste-t-il de la culture française?* (Paris: Denoël, 2008). See Oana Panaïté, 'Crise du français, impact de la francophonie?', *Alternative francophone*, 1:7 (2014), 1–11 (p. 1).

enrichment of French literature with 'linguistic zest from France's overseas territories, its former colonies, and other exotic climes', elements of what he sees as a wider 'ferment on the fringes',[26] he points to the interconnection of these two phenomena, revealing the flaws in his own polemical argument which points rather to the ways in which an official discourse of French culture has failed to understand the irreversible changes undergone by the object it seeks to encapsulate.

Harnessing the potential of such 'ferment', Francophone postcolonial studies has, since the turn of the millennium at least, sought to relativize and even provincialize metropolitan France within a wider Francospheric frame, whilst suggesting at the same time that the country has been reluctant, in Thomas Spear's terms, to 'se faire métisser par sa "propre" francophonie'.[27] Recent years have seen a mainstreaming of such an approach, for instance in the 2010 collection *French Global*, whose editors claim:

> Our contention is that such questions – about the tension between multiplicity and unity, between diversity and uniformity, between 'same' and 'other', as well as the related questions of migration and diasporic identities – are not limited to the emergence of 'Francophone literature'; rather, they have informed every period of French literature, starting with some of its most canonical texts.[28]

The same is true in postcolonial historiography, a precursor to which has recently been revealed in the belated publication of a project commissioned by UNESCO from Lucien Febvre and François Crouzet in 1950, but subsequently shelved,[29] the central thesis of which was that the French have always already been 'des sang-mêlés'. In this optic, France itself was always already a site of cultural hybridization, meaning that, as Nancy L. Green has recently noted, '[i]t is not just the impact of the *métropole* on the colonies but the impact of the colonies on the *métropole* that has stimulated new research in French history'.[30] Postcolonial

---

26. Morrison, *Death of French Culture*, pp. 75, 82.

27. *La Culture française vue d'ici et d'ailleurs: treize auteurs témoignent*, ed. by Thomas Spear (Paris: Karthala, 2002), p. 12. Marc Quaghebeur similarly argues that: 'L'heure devra venir pour la France de devenir la fille des Francophonies; d'en constituer une.' See 'Pour un enseignement pluriel et foncier des littératures francophones', in *Francophonies d'Europe, du Maghreb et du Machrek: littératures et libertés*, ed. by Marc Quaghebeur (Brussels: Peter Lang, 2013), pp. 185–208 (p. 193).

28. *French Global: A New Approach to Literary History*, ed. by Christie McDonald and Susan Rubin Suleiman (New York: Columbia University Press, 2010), p. xi.

29. Lucien Febvre and François Crouzet, *Nous sommes des sangs-mêlés: manuel d'histoire de la civilisation française*, ed. by Denis Crouzet and Elisabeth Crouzet (Paris: Albin Michel, 2012).

30. Nancy L. Green, 'French History and the Transnational Turn', *French Historical Studies*, 37:4 (2014), 551–64 (p. 555). Green's article includes a discussion of Febvre and Crouzet's book; see pp. 556–7.

approaches to history have suggested that France and its colonial territories did not exist in parallel, but demonstrate instead a symbiotic relationship according to which – in the terms of Emmanuelle Saada's argument – 'the Republic did not contradict itself in the colonies so much as it *revealed* its main internal tensions'.[31] As such, there is an increasing awareness of the co-existence and even interdependency of France and the rest of the French-speaking world, a shift whose logical implication is, in Dominick Lacapra's terms, that '[t]he turn to the francophone should in fact mean a turning of both the francophone and the metropolitan towards one another in order to elicit their tangled relations, their often lost opportunities, and their possibilities for the future'.[32] The acknowledgement of intra-francophone connections is further contextualized by the emerging transnational historiography, seen variously as 'histoire comparée, croisée, connectée, circulatoire, *entangled*, etc.',[33] which analyses, in an internationalized, multilingual frame, phenomena often seen (on a superficial or ideological level) to be quintessentially and homogeneously 'French' – and challenges as a result the assumptions of a nationalizing, centralizing 'Francodoxy'.[34] Todd Shepard's recent research on Algeria, France and Mexico, and the role of UNESCO in debates on anti-colonialism and decolonization, is exemplary in this regard, revealing the ways in which the French sought to manufacture an appearance of exceptionalism and to domesticate the Algerian War of Independence despite the overtly international context in which it occurred.[35]

In attempting to define the intellectual project underpinning French studies – and indeed Modern Languages more generally – Mary Louise Pratt's focus, in her 2002 reflection, on the 'importance of knowing languages and of knowing the world through languages' has often been cited.[36] Asking what is 'French' about French studies forces attenuation of Pratt's observation, not least in terms

---

31. Emmanuelle Saada, 'More than a Turn? The "Colonial" in French Studies', *French Politics, Culture and Society*, 32:2 (2014), 34–9 (p. 35).

32. Dominick Lacapra, *History and Reading: Tocqueville, Foucault, French Studies* (Toronto: University of Toronto Press, 2000), p. 225.

33. For a discussion of these terms, see Nancy L. Green, 'Le Transnationalisme et ses limites: le champ de l'histoire des migrations', in *Pratiques du transnational: terrains, preuves, limites,* ed. by Jean-Paul Zuñiga (Paris: La Bibliothèque du Centre de recherches historiques, 2011), pp. 197–208 (p. 198).

34. The idea of a 'Francodoxie' is developed by François Provenzano in *Vies et mort de la Francophonie: une politique française de la langue et de la littérature* (Brussels and Paris: Les Impressions Nouvelles, 2011).

35. Todd Shepard, 'Algeria, France, Mexico, UNESCO: A Transnational History of Anti-racism and Decolonization, 1932–1962', *Journal of Global History*, 6:2 (2011), 273–97.

36. Mary Louise Pratt, 'Building a new public idea about language', *Profession*, 2003, 110–19 (p. 112).

of: which languages? which world? and what forms of knowing? It is to these aspects that I turn in conclusion:

Languages

Although competence in the French language, and an awareness of multiple linguistic contexts, remains central to French studies, the traditional ethnolinguistic nationalism on which the area was founded, with the normative tendencies this implies, is increasingly untenable. This is part of what Alison Phipps has called a more general 'unmooring' of languages in the twenty-first century,[37] a situation generated in part by one of the key shifts inherent in the challenge of diversity, that is, a recognition that the historically monolingualizing tendencies of centralized states such as France have been increasingly challenged by a contemporary condition of post-monolingualism.[38] Jean-Marc Moura described, in *Littérature francophone et théorie postcoloniale*, the ways in which '[l]es études postcoloniales conçoivent plutôt le français comme une langue au pluriel, dépourvue de centre évident',[39] and in terms of the French language, the possibilities are double-edged. On the one hand, the diversification of objects of study, not least transculturally, permits exploration of a semiodiversity that scholars such as Claire Kramsch consider essential to the study of languages and cultures. In Kramsch's terms:

> Monolingualism is a handicap, but so is the assumption that one language = one culture = adherence to one cultural community. German culture speaks Turkish, Turkish culture speaks German. Spanish-speaking illegal immigrants in the U.S. are also Yucatec Maya or Guatemalan Indians who do not identify with any particular community, neither within nor outside the U.S. They have worldviews and express meanings that may differ from those of established communities. Monolingualism is the name not only for a linguistic handicap but for a dangerously monolithic traffic in meaning. The problem, as [Michael] Halliday said recently, is not a lack of glossodiversity but of semiodiversity.[40]

Kramsch's examples could be supplemented by equally valid ones from the Francosphere, evidence of her concluding observation that '[t]he role of the language teacher should be to diversify meanings, point to the meanings not chosen, and bring to light other possible meanings that have been forgotten by

37. Alison Phipps, 'Unmoored: Language Pain, Porosity, and Poisonwood', *Critical Multilingualism Studies*, 1:2 (2013), 96–118.

38. On post-monolingualism, see Yasemin Yildiz, *Beyond the Mother Tongue: The Post-Monolingual Condition* (New York: Fordham University Press, 2012).

39. Jean-Marc Moura, *Littérature francophone et théorie postcoloniale* (Paris: Presses universitaires de France, 1999), p. 7.

40. Claire Kramsch, 'The Traffic in Meaning', *Asia Pacific Journal of Education*, 5 (2006), 99–104 (p. 102).

history or covered up by politics'.[41] On the other, however, French is not only a language variegated in its usage, present as a world language, requiring, as a result, approaches that are more 'global and heterodox';[42] it is also a means of communication that exists in diglossic and polyglossic situations, not least in France itself, where it is subject to processes of translation, and also drawn into new linguistic and cultural phenomena such as creolization and translanguaging.

The foundational assumptions of French studies, despite their emphases on a degree of contrastive comparatism, risked replacing an Anglophone monolingual mind-set with a Francophone equivalent, normalizing monolingualism as what Elizabeth Ellis calls 'the unmarked case',[43] developing what Robert Young – in the context of single language departments and the institutional restriction of postcolonial comparatism – has called 'un système d'apartheid jalousement gardé',[44] and engaging in the 'dangerously monolithic traffic in meaning', accordingly ignoring the challenges of diversity, against which Kramsch cautions. As several contributors to the recent special issue of *French Politics, Culture and Society* on 'Flourishing in a Tough Climate' make clear, challenging the legacies of such a situation requires the acquisition of new languages, or at the very least initiation of collaborative activity that prizes open the residual monolingualism of the field.[45] This openness to a wider range of languages, or at the minimum to a variety of linguistic interconnections, is integral to a reconfiguration of the frames in which French studies operates, and one of the first steps towards this is – as David Damrosch suggests in a recent study of Julio Cortázar in France – recognition of the 'presence of the world within the nation'.[46] This does not mean that the French language – in its variegated forms and multiple interconnections – can no longer serve as a 'gravitational force for our entropic field',[47] but it requires in addition that the literary and otherwise verbally standardized elements of that language need to be relativized and understood in their complex interactions with

---

41. Kramsch, 'The Traffic in Meaning', p. 103.

42. Dubois and Mbembe, 'Nous sommes tous francophones', p. 42.

43. Elizabeth Ellis, 'Monolingualism: the Unmarked Case', *Estudios de sociolingüística: Linguas, sociedades e culturas*, 7:2 (2006), 173–96.

44. Robert J. C. Young, 'Littérature anglaise ou littératures en langue anglaise', in *Le Post-colonial comparé: Anglophonie, Francophonie*, ed. by Claire Joubert and Émilienne Baneth-Nouailhetas (Paris: Presses universitaires de Vincennes, 2014), pp. 45–59 (p. 45).

45. See for example Dubois and Mbembe, 'Nous sommes tous francophones', p. 42: 'Any student who wishes to do any serious work in Haiti needs a command of both Creole and French.'

46. David Damrosch, 'World Literature as Figure and as Ground', 'ACLA 2014–15 Report on the States of the Discipline of Comparative Literature', < http://stateofthediscipline. acla.org/entry/world-literature-figure-and-ground-0> [accessed 31 March 2015].

47. Herrick Chapman, 'Introduction: Flourishing in a Tough Climate', *French Politics, Culture and Society*, 32:2 (2014), 1–8 (p. 5).

non-verbal languages. This includes recognition of the importance of music and – as Leathes's report suggested almost a century ago – visual cultures; at the same time, it requires a more fundamental understanding of the meaning of what Betsy Rymes calls 'communicating beyond language' and acknowledging the complexity of wider 'communicative repertoires'.[48]

World

French studies might congratulate itself on its potential to challenge the a-linguistic tendencies of other disciplinary fields, but it has itself often shown 'a-mobile' tendencies through perpetuation of notions of spatial and cultural fixity.[49] Transnationalizing France is a first step,[50] but, as Bill Marshall suggests with his identification of a 'diasporic Frenchness',[51] it is clear that the 'French' in 'French studies' is increasingly determined by processes – within, beyond and across nation-spaces – of migration, return migration, travel and tourism, transnational circulation and diasporization, as well as by the spatial mobility of cultural objects, ideas and other non-human phenomena.[52] The world of French studies is accordingly one marked by the importance of mobility, challenging any regulation of knowledge according to what Brenner has dubbed the 'traditional Cartesian model of homogeneous, self-enclosed and contiguous blocks of territory'.[53]

Different frames are required to encompass such a revised understanding of the objects of study. François Provenzano has evoked a 'francophonie du "Nord"' to encapsulate an approach to France that highlights the axes linking it to Belgium and Quebec, suggesting an intra-francophone or franco-francophone comparatism that privileges what Marc Quaghebeur, in another context, has dubbed 'transversalités francophones'.[54] Increasingly, however, a wider Francosphere is

48. Betsy Rymes, *Communicating Beyond Language: Everyday Encounters with Diversity* (New York: Routledge, 2014).

49. On the risks of 'a-mobile' approaches, see Kevin Hannam, Mimi Sheller and John Urry, 'Editorial: Mobilities, Immobilities and Moorings', *Mobilities*, 1:1 (2006), 1–22 (p. 5).

50. On this subject, see Tyler Stovall, *Transnational France: The Modern History of a Universal Narrative* (Boulder, CO: Westview Press, 2015).

51. See Bill Marshall, *The French Atlantic: Travels in Culture and History* (Liverpool: Liverpool University Press, 2009).

52. For a more detailed discussion of these questions, see Charles Forsdick, 'Mobilizing French Studies', *Australian Journal of French Studies*, 48:1 (2011), 88–103.

53. N. Brenner, *New State Spaces: Urban Governance and the Rescaling of Statehood* (Oxford: Oxford University Press, 2004), p. 66. Cited in Hannam, Sheller and Urry, 'Editorial', p. 3.

54. François Provenzano, *Historiographies périphériques* (Brussels: Académie royale de Belgique, 2011); and Marc Quaghebeur, '"Francophone", le mot qu'il s'agit d'habiter enfin. Un entretien par Sabrina Parent', *ElFe XX-XXI*, 4 (2014), 171–81 (p. 175). These

the spatial paradigm that seems to encompass the geographical dimensions of the 'French' in French studies, deliberately selected as an alternative to the 'Francophone' or 'French-speaking' world to stress the fuzziness of that unit's boundaries, the asymmetrical power relationships it encompasses (neo-colonial formations and the nation-state persist), and the multicultural, transnational and polyglossic configurations it assumes.[55] The Francosphere implies the existence of spheres of influence, with France – as still the largest French-speaking country – often acting as a centre of gravity, but one 'displaced from the focal point of analysis and demoted to the status of a "case" among others – sometimes of particular interest because of the existence of unusually interesting French sources [. . .], sometimes marginalized as an outlier in a model that fits other states better'.[56] At the same time, whilst containing an assemblage of national spaces, the Francosphere also invites investigation of its intersections with other areas described by Christopher Bush, in the context of World Literature, as 'bigger than the nation, smaller than the world':

> oceanic (the Transatlantic; the Black Atlantic; various framings of the Pacific; most recently the Indian Ocean), continental (the Americas; Europe; Asia), imperial (Ottoman; Mongol; post-Soviet; Qing); linguistic (the Sinophone; the Sanskrit cosmopolis), and commercial (the silk road; the Mediterranean).[57]

In Bush's terms, such units – 'heterogeneous and [. . .] by no means mutually exclusive' – have an advantage particularly pertinent for those active in areas such as French studies: '[t]hey break open the limits of the national while retaining enough specificity to allow for in-depth research, knowledge of the relevant languages, and so on.' As such, they constitute part of a definitive

---

approaches are further developed through the concerted identification and analysis of other regions where a Francophone cultural substratum is evident, such as Central and Eastern Europe. On this subject, see *L'Autre Francophonie*, ed. by Joanna Nowicki and Catherine Mayaux (Paris: Honoré Champion, 2014).

55. Liverpool University Press launched, with the University of London Institute in Paris, a journal called *Francosphères* in 2012. Its mission statement outlines a commitment 'to define and question the presence of French language and culture across frontiers and borders, as defined by the Franco postcolonial presence, contact with French culture, and the "France of the mind". To this extent, it is a journal of transcultural and intercultural French Studies – about liminal spaces rather than operating within the hierarchy of "French" or "Francophone" culture'. See < http://francospheres.liverpooluniversitypress. co.uk/> [accessed 31 March 2015].

56. See Goldhammer, 'A Few Thoughts on the Future of French Studies', p. 18.

57. Christopher Bush, 'Areas: Bigger than the Nation, Smaller than the World', 'ACLA 2014–15 Report on the States of the Discipline of Comparative Literature', < http://stateofthediscipline.acla.org/entry/areas-bigger-nation-smaller-world> [accessed 31 March 2015].

challenge to the 'methodological nationalism' in the light of which French studies was established and allowed to evolve as an autonomous field,[58] and demonstrate the full potential of prizing open our understandings of 'French'. Such a manœuvre cannot but entail disruption to established practices and paradigms, challenging the remnants of any approach that transforms 'France and *la Francophonie* into a museum of aesthetic and ethnographic artifacts, treating France as a work of art, an aesthetically pleasing lifestyle which is reflected even in its government, institutions and economy, with Francophone studies added as a new wing to the French *musée imaginaire*'.[59]

Forms of knowing

In a searching exploration of the ideological underpinnings of the study of language and culture, Alastair Pennycook argues that 'we need to ask what meanings are being borne by languages, what cultural politics underlie the learning and use of different languages'.[60] The forms of knowing with which French studies is associated are never neutral, and what is not 'French' is the critical perspective that the field affords. Even within literature study, despite – as Malcolm Bowie demonstrated eloquently in his 1992 article – the contribution to a quintessentially French tradition of *lettres modernes* (and in particular to close textual scholarship),[61] the external gaze of Anglophone French studies has challenged, disrupted and ultimately contributed to the reorientation of narratives of literary history. The tradition of writing histories of literature in French outside France and the French-speaking world is strong, with Denis Hollier's 1989 *New History of French Literature* supplemented by Peter France's 1995 *New Oxford Companion to Literature in French*, and more recently by Christie McDonald and Susan Suleiman's 2010 *French Global*. This body of texts – two of which have been translated into French – exemplify a constructive, disruptive,

---

58. The term 'methodological nationalism' – designating the 'still-powerful nineteenth-century assumption that nations were the logical containers' for geographically-based enquiry – is used by Kenneth Pomeranz in 'Histories for a Less National Age', *American Historical Review*, 119:1 (2014), 1–22 (p. 2).

59. Watson, 'Culture and the Future of French Studies', p. 482. Marc Quaghebeur develops this argument in a reflection on principles that could be seen to underpin French studies in some of its earliest manifestations: 'L'invention de cet espace pluriel, qui devra être bien plus qu'un espace décentralisé, met évidemment en cause le modèle jacobin qui prévalut en France, mais aussi des formes de vision occidentales du monde telles que le XIXe siècle les véhicula au moment de l'essor majeur du processus colonial.' 'Pour un enseignement pluriel et foncier des littératures francophones', pp. 187–8.

60. Alastair Pennycook, 'Language Education as Translingual Activism', *Asia Pacific Journal of Education*, 26:1 (2006), 111–14 (p. 111).

61. Malcolm Bowie, 'Les Études françaises dans les universités britanniques'.

ethnographic perspective.[62] In Michael Kelly's terms, in the context of
French cultural studies, there is a specific value to a 'non-French perspective',
or what he dubs 'le regard de l'étranger'.[63] That such an approach is on occasion
rejected – as was the case with postcolonial studies, particularly in the work
of Jean-Loup Amselle and Jean-François Bayart,[64] and also with cultural studies,
in the dismissal of 'les ruses de la raison impérialiste' by Pierre Bourdieu
and Loïc Wacquant –[65] is an indication of its power; it suggests that, although
there might be key thinkers who have inspired some of the finest scholarship
in French studies – de Beauvoir, Deleuze, Derrida, Durkheim, Fanon, Foucault,
Glissant, Irigaray, Lévi-Strauss, Mauss, Sartre, Stiegler and many others – and
that although there might be 'francophone' paradigms that have influenced
our approaches – including the historiographic *syndrome*, *mythologies*, *lieux de
mémoire*, *Tout-Monde*, *littérature-monde*, *l'intraduisible* – the anglicization of
the field proposed back in 1918, the rejection of any mimetic impulse, remains a
disciplinary strength.

In an article on contemporary French studies in the USA, Véronique Maisier
lists the various sub-disciplinary labels whereby the study of French and French-
speaking cultures may now be designated: 'études françaises/ francophones/
francopolyphoniques/ francosphériques',[66] to which we might also add other
neologisms such as 'francographes'. If we allow this proliferation of terms to
generate a divisive taxonomic anxiety, then the fragility of our area of study is
further exacerbated; if, however, we turn the 'becoming-transnational' of the
increasingly porous and diversified 'French' in 'French studies' into a defining

---

62. *A New History of French literature*, ed. by Denis Hollier (Cambridge, MA: Harvard
    University Press, 1989); *The New Oxford Companion to Literature in French*, ed. by Peter
    France (Oxford: Oxford University Press, 1995). The volumes edited by Hollier and by
    McDonald and Suleiman were translated, respectively, as *De la littérature française*
    (Paris: Bordas, 1993) and *French Global: une nouvelle perspective sur l'histoire littéraire*
    (Paris: Classiques Garnier, 2014).

63. Michael Kelly, '*Le Regard de l'étranger*: What French Cultural Studies Brings to French
    Cultural History', *French Cultural Studies*, 25:3/4 (2014), 253–61.

64. Jean-Loup Amselle, *L'Occident décroché: enquête sur les postcolonialismes* (Paris:
    Stock, 2008), and Jean-François Bayart, 'En finir avec les études postcoloniales',
    Le Débat, 154 (2009), 119–40. A version of Bayart's article was included in English
    translation as 'Postcolonial Studies: A Political Invention of Tradition?' in an issue of
    Public Culture devoted to 'Racial France', guest-edited by Janet Roitman (23.1 (2011);
    Bayart's piece is pp. 55–84). In this context, it was robustly critiqued by other con-
    tributors such as Achille Mbembe ('Provincializing France?', pp. 85–119) and Robert
    J. C. Young ('Bayart's Broken Kettle', pp. 167–75).

65. Pierre Bourdieu and Loïc Wacquant, 'On the Cunning of Imperialist Reason', *Theory,
    Culture and Society*, 16:1 (2000), 41–58.

66. Véronique Maisier, 'L'État des études françaises, francophones et globales dans les
    universités américaines', *Alternative francophone*, 1:7 (2014), 12–24 (p. 21).

strength rather than a sign of fragmentation, then the sub-field has the opportunity to retain a coherent focus whilst locating itself in relation to Modern Languages (and indeed a wider set of fields in the Humanities and Social Sciences).[67] Just as José Saldívar has proposed a concept of 'trans-Americanity' that would allow a move from 'acting and thinking from the nation-state level' towards 'thinking and acting at the planetary and world-systems level',[68] so a 'trans-Francophone' approach might similarly encourage a productive engagement across such a wide range of levels of granularity, allowing what Arthur Goldhammer calls a 'reflective equilibrium between the local and the global, in which even more intimate knowledge of the part fosters deeper insight into the workings of the whole'.[69] In 1992, Malcolm Bowie already described the threats to French studies of a 'nouvelle forme de mercantilisme philistin qui nous entoure',[70] and there is now a greater threat than ever that the scope and methodology of French studies in the twenty-first century will be market-driven and dictated by an instrumentalization of languages increasingly prevalent in the undergraduate curriculum. In such a model, what is 'French' about French studies risks being defined regressively and restrictedly in national and almost exclusively linguistic terms. Marc Quaghebeur states: 'L'Espace francophone sera pluriel ou il disparaîtra,'[71] suggesting that engagement with such an object of study requires '[u]ne conscience transversale, plus ou moins largement métissée'.[72] If the 'French' in French studies is defined along such lines – encapsulating, contextualizing, historicizing as well as 'languaging' the often unpredictable transnational interconnections and complex politico-cultural reconfigurations of the twenty-first century – then the field might discern new focus, impetus and direction by privileging its engagement with the challenges of diversity.[73]

---

67. The term 'becoming-transnational' is used by Françoise Lionnet; see 'Introduction', in *Francophone Studies: New Landscapes*, ed. by Françoise Lionnet and Dominic Thomas (*Modern Language Notes*, 118:4 (2003)), 783–6 (p. 784).

68. José Saldívar, *Trans-Americanity: Subaltern Modernities, Global Coloniality and the Cultures of Greater Mexico* (Durham, NC: Duke University Press, 2012), p. xvii.

69. Goldhammer, 'A Few Thoughts on the Future of French Studies', p. 20.

70. Bowie, 'Les Études françaises dans les universités britanniques', p. 87.

71. Quaghebeur, 'Pour un enseignement pluriel et foncier des littératures francophones', p. 185.

72. Marc Quaghebeur, 'Comment sortir de l'Un qui hante et paralyse les Francophonies', in *Les Interculturalités: état des lieux et perspectives, théories et pratiques*, ed. by Cynthia Eid and Fady Fadel (Brussels: EME, 2014), pp. 201–16 (p. 216).

73. This article was completed while I was Arts and Humanities Research Council Theme Leadership Fellow for 'Translating Cultures' (AH/K503381/1); I record my thanks to the AHRC for its support.

Nottingham French Studies 54.3 (2015): 328–339
DOI: 10.3366/nfs.2015.0130
© University of Nottingham
www.euppublishing.com/journal/nfs

LA FRANCE N'A PAS ÉTÉ AU RENDEZ-VOUS

AZOUZ BEGAG

Introduction d'Alec G. Hargreaves

À la fin du colloque tenu à l'Université de Nottingham le 21 mars 2015 autour du dossier publié en 1985 par *Le Figaro magazine* « Serons-nous encore français dans 30 ans? », Azouz Begag a été invité à apporter son témoignage personnel à partir de sa triple carrière, qui a traversé l'ensemble de cette période. Celle de socio-économiste spécialisé dans l'étude des populations immigrées en milieux urbains a donné lieu à son premier livre en 1984,[1] puis à de nombreux articles et essais, alimentés par ses recherches au CNRS. Celle d'écrivain commence en 1986 par *Le Gone du Chaâba*,[2] un roman inspiré par son enfance à Lyon où il est né en 1957, de parents immigrés algériens. Begag a aujourd'hui à son actif une vingtaine de romans, ainsi que plusieurs scénarios de cinéma et de bandes dessinées. Tout en poursuivant ses carrières de chercheur et d'écrivain, il s'investit dans une troisième voie, celle de citoyen engagé, qui l'amènera à servir comme Ministre délégué à l'égalité des chances dans le gouvernement de Dominique de Villepin de 2005 à 2007. Il est aujourd'hui Conseiller Culturel de l'Ambassade de France au Portugal et Directeur de l'Institut Français de Lisbonne.

Ma première rencontre avec Azouz Begag remonte au début des trois décennies qui se sont écoulées depuis le dossier du *Figaro magazine*. C'était en 1987. Je l'avais interviewé alors dans le cadre d'un ouvrage que je préparais sur les écrivains « beurs »[3]. Depuis lors, nous avons travaillé ensemble à de multiples reprises et nous ne nous sommes jamais perdus de vue, en Europe comme aux États-Unis[4]. Durant cette période, nous avons partagé nos inquiétudes sur les effets néfastes des discriminations subies par les minorités postcoloniales en France.

Les conséquences de ces discriminations ont évolué avec le temps. Les travailleurs immigrés, la plupart du temps analphabètes, non francophones et

---

1. *L'Immigré et sa ville* (Presses Universitaires de Lyon, 1984).
2. *Le Gone du Chaâba* (Paris: Seuil, 1986).
3. Alec G. Hargreaves, *Voices from the North African Immigrant Community in France: Immigration and Identity in Beur Fiction* (Oxford and New York: Berg, 1991).
4. « Azouz Begag et Alec Hargreaves: entretien sur un quart de siècle de collaboration », propos recueilles par Sarah Glasco, *Expressions maghrébines*, 11:1 (2012), 159–80.

pauvres, venus combler les pénuries de main d'œuvre pendant les trente glorieuses subissaient en silence les comportements discriminatoires, confortés par la perspective d'un retour au pays d'origine. Des enfants sont nés de ces parents immigrés. Ils ont atteint l'âge adulte au cours des années 1970, quand les chocs pétroliers provoquaient une crise économique sévère sans précédent et créaient du chômage. Contrairement à leurs parents, les membres de cette nouvelle génération – celle d'Azouz Begag – se croient destinés à s'intégrer dans la société française, et devenir français. Ils ont appris la culture et les valeurs dominantes en France sur les bancs de l'école républicaine. C'est en leur nom qu'ils organisent en 1983 une première grande manifestation demandant la fin des discriminations dont ils sont les victimes. En guise de réponse, tout en tenant un discours grandiloquent sur les valeurs républicaines, les pouvoirs publics agiront peu pour réprimer ces discriminations.

Dans le deuxième roman de Begag, *Béni ou le paradis perdu,* le protagoniste éponyme tombe amoureux d'une jeune fille blonde appelée (avec un évident symbolisme) France. Elle lui donne rendez-vous dans une boîte de nuit nommée *le Paradis de la nuit.* On ne le laissera pas entrer. Son exclusion, pour des motifs racistes, empêche Béni de réaliser son rêve: rejoindre France. Elle provoque chez lui une violente colère, la haine:

> J'ai dit mille fois « enculé de votre mère » et tous les gros mots, les mots énormes, les mots immenses qui se cachaient dans mes tiroirs de garçon respectueux sont sortis comme du vomi de ma bouche. En crachant sur leur mère, je me suis juré de revenir le lendemain pour mettre le feu à ce Paradis de merde.[5]

Cette réaction violente nous fait pressentir l'émergence dans les années 1990 d'une troisième vague de Maghrébins et d'autres minorités postcoloniales qui, face à l'inertie des pouvoirs publics devant les discriminations qu'ils subissent, ne croient déjà plus aux promesses de la République et sont tentés par des comportements déviants et violents qui dans cas extrêmes se transforment en actes terroristes.

En 1995, alors que l'Algérie est en pleine guerre civile, en France, le jeune Khaled Kelkal, 21 ans, et des amis qui ont grandi en banlieue lyonnaise participent aux premiers attentats commis en France par des jeunes issus de l'immigration. Dans la foulée, Jacques Chirac se rend à Lyon pour rencontrer des acteurs du terrain susceptibles de l'éclaircir sur les racines du mal. Le reportage de cette rencontre publié dans *Le Monde* commence avec les propos suivants de Chirac:

> « Alors, là, votre histoire de boîte de nuit, ça me sidère! » Au cours de sa rencontre avec le maire, les représentants de la communauté musulmane, le Père Christian Delorme, et des associations de Vaulx-en-Velin, jeudi 12 octobre, Jacques Chirac a

---

5. *Béni ou le paradis perdu* (Paris: Seuil, 1989), p. 171.

paru étonné lorsqu'Azouz Begag, lui a expliqué avec des anecdotes la discrimination raciale dont souffrent les jeunes des cités.

« Nous, avec nos gueules d'Arabes, on est visibles à l'entrée d'une boîte de nuit.
On nous refuse l'entrée. On nous dit: "C'est complet!" alors qu'on fait entrer
d'autres clients! » « Mais enfin, » aurait dit le président, « il y a quelques semaines,
j'ai rencontré une soixantaine de jeunes d'origine maghrébine et africaine dans un
quartier du Havre. Jamais ils ne m'ont dit qu'ils avaient été mis à la porte d'une
boîte de nuit! » « C'est normal, Monsieur le Président: Ils ne peuvent pas être mis à
la porte d'une boîte de nuit puisque, déjà, ils ne peuvent pas y entrer! », a répondu
l'écrivain.[6]

Malgré son apparent intérêt pour les problèmes soulevés par Azouz Begag,
Chirac sera peu enclin aux actions concrètes contre les discriminations. Ce n'est
qu'en juin 2005, soit dix ans plus tard et sous la pression d'une directive
européenne, qu'il inaugure la Haute Autorité de lutte contre les discriminations
et pour l'égalité, dénoncée par un collectif de mouvements antiracistes comme
un « projet en trompe l'œil » conçu pour « répondre de manière minimaliste
aux obligations européennes [...], un pur effet d'annonce visant à masquer
l'absence de volonté politique de prendre les mesures radicales qu'exige la lutte
contre les discriminations »[7]. Les émeutes d'octobre et novembre 2005 – les
désordres les plus importants survenus en France en quarante ans – témoignent de
la profondeur des injustices ressenties par les jeunes des banlieues et de l'absence
de volonté des politiques pour les corriger.

Quelques mois plus tôt, juste avant sa nomination au gouvernement
de Dominique de Villepin, Azouz Begag avait achevé un manuscrit intitulé
Les Jeunes Ethniques dans lequel il décrivait l'aggravation du désespoir des
minorités postcoloniales et les risques de déflagration sociopolitique pour la
société française. Une traduction anglaise de ce manuscrit, resté inédit en France,
est publiée aux États-Unis en 2007. On y lit:

It will take years to repair the consequences of decades of political neglect. During
the period immediately following the Second World War, the French enjoyed what
they came to look back on nostalgically as *les trente glorieuses*, thirty glorious years
of economic expansion and near-full employment. During that period, economic
migrants were actively sought in response to labor shortages in France. Many came
from colonial or former colonial territories in Africa and elsewhere. The economic
slowdown which began with the oil shocks of the 1970s gave rise to what I call *les
trente calamiteuses*, thirty disastrous years of high unemployment and economic
insecurity in which the children and grand-children of migrants, especially those

6.   Dominique Le Guilledoux, « "Votre histoire de boîte de nuit, ça me sidère"! », *Le Monde*,
       14 octobre 1995.
7.   Collectif pour une autorité indépendante universelle de lutte contre les discriminations,
       « Projet de loi HALDE: Une autorité pour rien ? », 4 octobre 2004, < http://www.
       gisti.org> [consulté le 8 octobre 2004].

originating in the Islamic world, were treated as suspect or illegitimate parts of French society. It is now time to inaugurate *les trente prometteuses*, thirty promising years for which it is our responsibility to prepare the way by removing the obstacles and injustices placed in the path of minority ethnic citizens. A France which turns its back on diversity is a nation unfaithful to the principles of the Republic. A Republic which embraces and celebrates diversity is the harbinger of a richer and stronger France.[8]

Compte tenu des attentats terroristes de janvier 2015 à Paris – les plus meurtriers survenus en France depuis plus d'un demi-siècle – j'ai posé à Begag la question suivante: « Dix ans après *Les Jeunes Ethniques* et les émeutes de 2005, qu'en est-il de l'idée des trente prometteuses? C'est un mythe? C'est un leurre? C'est fini? Est-ce que nous allons plutôt vers un prolongement des trente calamiteuses? » Ses réponses sont retranscrites ci-dessous.

Propos d'Azouz Begag

Je pense qu'on ne peut plus penser d'une manière linéaire … faire une continuité entre les trente glorieuses, 1945–75, les trente calamiteuses, 1975–2005, et le reste, 2005–2035 … parce que la France, depuis le 7 janvier 2015, n'est plus jamais, ne sera plus jamais la même. C'est quelque chose d'autre. Donc l'idée de la France s'est irrémédiablement modifiée le 7 janvier 2015, le jour de l'attentat contre *Charlie Hebdo*. Ainsi, le calcul que j'avais conçu sur la base des périodes de 30 ans n'est plus valable … mais ce n'est pas de mon fait …

Après les trente glorieuses, les trente calamiteuses, les autorités avaient une *alternative*, c'était de dire: « OK, nous avons compris, nous allons mettre tous les moyens à disposition d'une intégration réelle, d'une égalité des chances réelle … ou bien Le Pen va gagner! » … Et nous sommes en train de voir ce qui se passe: c'est Marine Le Pen qui va gagner … Entre le pire et le meilleur, c'est le pire qui va gagner … parce que c'est le plus facile à réaliser! C'est très simple de couper un arbre, mais faire grandir un arbre, ça prend un siècle … donc c'est le plus facile qui va gagner, c'est-à-dire le pire. Pendant un certain temps, tout au moins … Il n'y a pas de quoi être optimiste, mais pas de quoi être pessimiste, non plus, parce que dans deux siècles, d'autres colloques se passeront à Nottingham, avec d'autres personnes, peut-être nous ne serons plus là, et le monde continuera …

Alec Hargreaves et moi nous avions une prétention, nous voulions lutter contre la descente aux enfers de la République, de la France que nous aimons … Nous n'avons pas réussi. Alors, nous nous demandons, Catherine et Yvan[9] et tous les

---

8.   Azouz Begag, *Ethnicity and Equality: France in the Balance*, trad. par Alec G. Hargreaves (Lincoln: University of Nebraska Press, 2007), p. xxviii.

9.   Catherine Wihtol de Wenden et Yvan Gastaut étaient parmi les intervenants au colloque de l'Université de Nottingham.

chercheurs...: « à quoi servons-nous? » Nous avons dépensé beaucoup d'argent public pour comprendre les mécanismes du rejet, du racisme, de la violence ... pour ne pas en arriver là. Nous avons perdu ... Parce que nous n'avons pas été capables d'expliquer aux gens ... Quels gens? Je pense à ceux qui votent. c'était à eux qu'il fallait aller parler ... pour ne pas les laisser se faire embrigader par l'extrême-droite ... Nous, les chercheurs, les scientifiques, les intellectuels, si seulement nous avions pu frapper à la porte des gens et leur faire partager le fruit de nos recherches, de nos réflexions ... Nous n'avons pas réussi à le faire. Mais les prédicateurs musulmans ont fait ça, et les candidats du Front national l'ont fait aussi ... Faute de relais dans les médias et dans les milieux politiques, nous donnons parfois l'impression d'être restés, nous, protégés, derrière des portes blindées, avec des codes d'accès, avec nos théories et nos concepts, à l'université de Nottingham et ailleurs ...[10] Nous avons là perdu la bataille de la communication. À quoi sert le financement de la recherche publique, si ses résultats ne sont pas utilisés par le système politique ...

Il y a trente ans, nous avions déjà vu des jeunes dans les banlieues qui n'avaient plus rien à perdre ... Ils avaient appris, en France, que faire peur c'est exister politiquement. Faire peur, c'est exister! Si tu menaces, tu vas obtenir des choses ... mais si tu es trop gentil, trop silencieux, tu n'auras rien. Faire peur, c'est exister ... cela veut dire que le système d'exclusion en France, tel qu'il existe depuis cinquante ans, a valorisé la violence comme objet de négociation politique dans les cités ...

Une autre chose importante est à signaler ... La Marche dite des « Beurs », en fait une marche pour l'égalité et contre le racisme[11] a été ethnicisée par les journalistes pour dire que ce sont des jeunes ethniques qui ont fait ça. C'est comme si on disait aujourd'hui que l'action de Martin Luther King était essentiellement une marche de noirs! Ce qui est faux. Vous avez vu sur le pont de Selma, *the bridge,* à Selma, récemment dans le film *Selma* consacré à Luther King, il y a une diversité de visages et de couleurs qui manifeste contre la ségrégation. Dans notre marche pour l'égalité aussi, il y avait cette diversité, mais on l'a ethnicisée, alors qu'elle était politique et sociale ... C'est là le début de la grande manipulation.

La naissance des « Jeunes ethniques » se passait au début des années 80. Pour vous faire comprendre, sentir, ce que je veux dire, essayez de vous imaginer,

---

10. Begag joue ici de manière humoristique sur le système de sécurité en vigueur dans le bâtiment où s'est tenu le colloque de l'Université de Nottingham, dont l'accès était régi par un code confidentiel.

11. La Marche pour l'égalite et contre le racisme, qui a eu lieu à l'automne de 1983, a été couramment désignée par les médias comme la Marche des Beurs, ce qui a fait entrer dans le langage courant le mot « Beurs » pour désigner la deuxième génération des Maghrébins en France.

moi, Azouz, 20 ans, Lyonnais, avec une amie qui s'appelle France, à l'entrée d'une discothèque, où il y a une vingtaine de personnes qui attendent, des jeunes. Ils sont devant le videur. Celui qui « vide ». Ou alors, le nettoyeur, le purificateur. Cela se passe il y a trente ans, peut-être plus, quarante … Ce videur ouvre la porte et dit en montrant du doigt certains d'entre nous: « toi, toi, toi, pas la peine … » Les jeunes qui étaient ainsi désignés étaient des Noirs, des Arabes … parfois même des Juifs aussi, des Juifs séfarades, d'Algérie, qui étaient pris pour des Arabes. Je me souviens que mes amis juifs avaient fini par insister sur le fait qu'ils n'étaient pas arabes, pour qu'on fasse la différence … Et le videur disait, en ce qui concernait tous les autres qui protestaient: « Non, la réponse est non, dégagez de l'entrée. » On ne pouvait pas entrer dans la discothèque, pour la simple raison que « c'était comme ça! » Vous imaginez, nous, avec nos amis, l'humiliation! L'humiliation!

Voilà pourquoi … je ne dis pas comme Zlatan Ibrahimović, le joueur de l'équipe de Paris-Saint-Germain en colère …[12] mais je suis très en colère, quarante ans après avoir cru en la France et ses promesses républicaines, je crie à ce pays: « Pourquoi tu nous as fait ça? Regarde, maintenant, le résultat! Pourquoi tu n'as pas écouté, entendu ceux qui t'aimaient? »

J'ai beaucoup voyagé grâce aux ailes de mes livres … J'aime les Maoris de Nouvelle-Zélande … Les Maoris, 15% de la population totale de Nouvelle-Zélande, mais plus de 50% de la population carcérale … J'aime aussi les Noirs-Américains. Je me suis toujours considéré comme « leur frère ». Ils sont 14% de la population nord-américaine, mais 50% de la population carcérale … Et nous, nous, les « Ethniques » en France, nous sommes aussi 15% de la population totale et plus de 50% de la population en prison … quelle coïncidence, cette similitude! Le jour où j'ai vu ces chiffres dans une revue de Nouvelle-Zélande consacrée aux minorités ethniques dans ce pays, j'ai été surpris de constater ces proportions identiques en France, USA … C'est troublant. Cela montre parfaitement que la maltraitance sociale des minorités ethniques … quelles que soient les origines … est due aux discriminations qu'elles subissent dans l'éducation, l'emploi, la politique, la justice … alors qu'il y a ici et là une tendance à les rendre « responsables » de leurs malheurs! C'est un comble.

Ce que je veux dire c'est que ce système d'oppression peut rendre fous les plus faibles, les plus démunis, ceux qui n'ont rien à perdre. Drogues, alcool, maladies psychiatriques, violence contre soi, contre les femmes … sont le lot des plus vulnérables, partout dans le monde …

Ici en France, les enfants de l'immigration ont dit pendant les années 80–90: « Madame la France, si tu ne m'aimes pas, je vais me suicider, et après, c'est toi

---

12. Footballeur international suédois né de parents bosniaque-croate qui joue depuis 2012 pour Paris Saint-Germain. En mars 2015 il s'indigne de ce qu'il perçoit comme des erreurs d'arbitrage en qualifiant la France de « pays de merde ».

que je vais suicider … » Voilà ce que je voyais il y a trente ans, déjà … Des jeunes qui étaient prêts à se suicider lors de ce que j'appelais des rites sacrificiels. Ils ont commencé avec les rodéos, dans les quartiers avec des voitures de forte puissance … Les rodéos étaient suicidaires, déjà … C'est-à-dire, les jeunes se mettaient en danger de mort eux-mêmes, et dans leur quartier, aux yeux du monde entier. Alors je comprenais déjà que si ces jeunes étaient capables de mourir, ils pouvaient également tuer n'importe qui facilement. Leur vie ne valait rien! « Alors, la vôtre, encore moins! », ils nous disaient …

Moi, j'ai eu la chance d'avoir accès à l'éducation, avoir des outils, un recours intellectuel, pour surmonter l'humiliation devant les discothèques, celle vécue au moment où j'apprends que les agences immobilières ne veulent pas louer à des Arabes, les injures raciales, les violences des policiers … oui, j'ai eu la chance de faire de l'humiliation subie une force d'écriture, de réaction, de survie … de compréhension. Mais dans les quartiers où j'ai grandi, j'étais minoritaire. Beaucoup de mes copains sont devenus fous. Beaucoup sont allés en prison …

Mais les années sont passées très vite. Qui se souvient encore de ce que nous avons vécu? Je voudrais maintenant évoquer quelque chose de très important: la mémoire collective, politique et sociale. Elle est un enjeu majeur d'une politique d'intégration des minorités. *Le Gone du Chaâba*, mon premier roman, est le début de la construction de ce type de mémoire collective chez les jeunes issus de l'immigration maghrébine … Une mémoire écrite, c'est important de le dire, parce que 90% des travailleurs immigrés du Maghreb en France étaient analphabètes. Ils ne savaient pas lire, pas écrire. Par conséquent, la seule transmission d'une mémoire maghrébine par nos parents, c'était l'oralité … Et nous, nous sommes nés en France et nous avons appris à lire et écrire à l'école républicaine. Nous avions accès aux livres. Au début des années 80, c'est la première fournée de romans littéraires, souvent autobiographiques, qui a commencé à créer une mémoire collective. Mais cette mémoire collective a été spoliée par le mouvement « SOS-Racisme », c'est-à-dire, par les idéologues de la politique, membres ou proches du Parti Socialiste, au tout début des mouvements collectifs de jeunes issus de l'immigration maghrébine dans les cités … voilà la cruelle réalité…. Cruelle pour nous, pour eux aussi … Ils ont volé la mémoire des jeunes des banlieues. Tout simplement. C'est très clair. Ils nous ont volé nos combats, notre capital mémoriel … Parmi eux, il y avait Bernard-Henri Lévy, Harlem Désir, Julien Dray … qui étaient des professionnels de la politique et qui ont vu dans ce mouvement de la Marche pour l'égalité et contre le racisme une belle occasion de prospérer, après l'élection de François Mitterrand à l'Elysée en 1981. Ils ont siphonné la mémoire d'une génération de jeunes des cités dont c'était la première expérience collective de revendication dans la société française … On peut considérer qu'aujourd'hui, la France paie le prix de ce hold-up historique, qui a empêché les jeunes des cités de se constituer en force politique, avec leur propre histoire, leur propre revendication, leur propre mémoire. Ils auraient pu devenir des « politiques », au sens noble du terme, apprendre les codes de ce métier, jouer le jeu républicain, en France, où ils sont nés. On les en a empêchés. Ils étaient plus légitimes que les autres!

Un jour, je disais à un jeune chômeur lors d'une réunion: « C'est très important d'avoir la mémoire, de savoir qui tu es, d'où tu viens, qui sont tes ancêtres.» Et d'une manière surprenante, il me répondit: « À quoi ça sert d'avoir de la mémoire quand on n'a pas d'avenir? » ... Je n'oublierai jamais cet échange. Ce jeune me paraissait enfermé dans le temps présent. Sans passé, sans futur. Il était comme errant, solitaire, dans l'espace-temps social ... je pense à lui, car je me dis qu'en allant proposer à des jeunes comme lui les services d'une « famille », les religieux musulmans prosélytes pouvaient facilement lever des armées ...

Le résultat du hold-up mémoriel par SOS-Racisme a eu une grave conséquence auprès des jeunes des cités. Ils ont compris que la France ne leur fera jamais de cadeau, et que pour exister socialement, il fallait lui faire peur politiquement, faire du bruit dans la cité pour négocier avec les autorités la paix sociale. Ils sont entrés dans une espèce de bras de fer avec la République.

Dépossédés de leur propre mémoire, les jeunes des cités ont été ensuite condamnés par un second coup, par la rhétorique sur la « victimisation ». À chaque fois que vous voulez évoquer le racisme dont vous êtes victime, dire par exemple: « Je ne peux pas rentrer dans les discothèques, trouver du travail, un logement, à cause du racisme ... », on vous assène: « Oh, stoppe ton discours de victimisation, on en a marre de vos plaintes. » C'est terrible! Même l'espace minimal de la liberté d'expression a été verrouillé par ce mot terrible, « victimisation » ... on peut aisément comprendre que la porte a été ouverte ainsi à la violence individuelle et collective ...

Tout cela veut dire que le silence doit être la règle d'or pour s'intégrer ... en plus de l'invisibilité ... (« sois belle et tais-toi! ») ... Ainsi, on voit que tous les « héros » issus de l'immigration qui prospèrent dans les médias, le sport, la télévision, la politique..., sont ceux qui ne parlent pas, qui ne sont pas, comme on dit si bien, « dans la revendication ».[13] Ils ne dérangent pas la société. Ils font croire que si on veut s'en sortir, on peut ... on n'a qu'à se donner les moyens ...

Voilà le contexte dans lequel l'islam comme famille, l'islam comme fraternité, comme mémoire collective, comme communauté où l'on est pleinement accueilli sans discrimination, est arrivé par les prisons ... C'est ce que racontait Khaled Kelkal, jeune terroriste des banlieues de Lyon tué en 1995.[14] ...En passant, il faut rappeler qu'aux États-Unis, c'est exactement ce qui s'est passé dans les années soixante avec *the Nation of Islam* et Malcolm X ... ce qui s'est produit avec les Noirs américains il y a cinquante ans ... C'est bizarre! On a l'impression que

---

13. Zinedine Zidane, capitaine de l'équipe de France qui a remporté le Mondial du football en 1998.

14. « Moi, Khaled Kelkal », propos recueillis par Dietmar Loch, *Le Monde*, 7 octobre 1995.

l'histoire des minorités en France, elle se répète comme aux États-Unis, mêmes causes, mêmes effets … quel que soit le pays où elle se passe. La Marche pour l'égalité et contre le racisme n'a-t-elle pas été copiée sur celle de Martin Luther King et du mouvement des Droits civiques? …

Ainsi, l'Islam … celui de l'imam du coin, en tout cas … a servi sur un plateau à une partie de la jeunesse d'origine maghrébine une idée de soi-même, une dignité, une force. C'est ça. Après le hold-up de leur mémoire, la religion apparaissait comme une bouée de secours dans la République des incantations vaines. Khaled Kelkal y croyait. Il est passé aux armes, en défendant tout ce qui lui restait, c'est-à-dire une idée de lui dans le monde …

Mon père est arrivé en France au début des années 50 sans parler un mot de français. La France lui a demandé de venir pour sa force physique, simplement, sans sa tête, ses pensées, elle n'en avait pas besoin dans les usines de montage … et, en vous écoutant aujourd'hui, je me suis rendu compte que le capitalisme n'est pas raciste. Il se moque des différences, au contraire, si elles peuvent le nourrir il va les vanter sans états d'âme … Nos parents étaient venus là pour travailler, ils n'avaient de légitimité que dans l'usine, nulle part ailleurs … Allah était dans leur cœur … et dans le titre racoleur du *Figaro-magazine* « Serons-nous encore français dans 30 ans? » … alors qu'aujourd'hui, la question de l'islam est partout dans l'espace public, celle du djihadisme en banlieue omniprésente, traumatisante … et, dans le même temps, on trouve dans les grands supermarchés de France des espaces réservés à la nourriture Hallal … parce que c'est une énorme source de profit! … Alors les supermarchés comme Casino, Carrefour, pendant la fête de *Ramadan,* gagnent beaucoup d'argent avec le commerce ethnique … Cela change beaucoup la question de l'intégration par rapport aux années 80.

Dans le sport aussi … Par exemple, si un jeune des cités, musulman et/ou noir, est un excellent joueur de football, s'il peut faire gagner son équipe, son nom, Zidane, Benzema, Varane, Thierry Henry, Gaël Monfils … ou récemment Fékir?[15], ne constituera jamais un obstacle à son intégration. Pas plus que sa couleur de peau … C'est d'ailleurs pourquoi la porte de l'intégration des jeunes des banlieues par le sport a été la principale durant des décennies … La société a dit à ces gens: « Voter, ça ne sert à rien. Laissez-nous la politique, on s'en occupe. Jouer au football! Soyez sportif, là vous gagnerez de l'argent, on vous respectera, vous trouverez une place … » Voilà ce qu'elle a dit, la société et voilà aussi pourquoi je suis en faveur du vote obligatoire … Une fois que les gens sont dans l'obligation de voter, ils vont être vus différemment, avec considération, par les candidats aux élections. Ils vont peser dans la balance … C'est pour ça qu'on veut leur faire croire: pas la politique! On leur a fait croire que c'était

---

15. Nabil Fékir, footballeur né à Lyon de parents immigrés algériens qui a choisi de jouer pour l'équipe nationale de France plutôt que pour l'équipe algérienne.

un domaine réservé aux membres de la majorité ... On les a empêchés de s'en mêler ... accusant de « communautarisme » toute tentative d'organisation de force politique dans les quartiers ... Conséquence, il y a aujourd'hui à l'Assemblée nationale, seulement deux députés issus de l'immigration maghrébine ... sur 577! ... et seulement 5 maires de communes d'origine maghrébine sur 36.000! ... dont depuis trois ans, le maire de Stains, dans la banlieue parisienne, trente-cinq mille habitants. Trente-six mille maires ... cinq seulement ... à comparer avec les 50–60% de ceux qui constituent la population en prison ... Qu'est-ce qui n'a pas marché en France depuis 50 ans dans l'intégration? ... les réponses sont là ... Le système politique dans son ensemble a décrépi ...

Au fond, oui ... nous n'avons pas eu de chance ... Moi, j'essayais d'entrer dans les discothèques pour rencontrer des Françaises, j'étais pour ... très favorable aux « rencontres interculturelles » ... mais on ne nous laissait pas entrer! c'était si frustrant et humiliant..., tandis que mon père, comme tous les autres, quand ils sont venus en France ... le paradis ... ils avaient dans la tête une idée, celle de rentrer au pays aussi tôt que possible. Ils ne se voyaient qu'en transit, en France où il y a du travail partout ... là, chez l'ancien colon, ils pouvaient se construire un futur, enfin, après la guerre d'indépendance, après la misère ... quand je repense à cette misère qu'ils ont vécue, les larmes me montent aux yeux ... Alors, le mythe du retour, c'était leur façon de survivre à l'éloignement, aux douleurs de l'exil ... bâtir une maison ... trois étages, avec garage et télévision ... Mais nous, les enfants, en France, nous étions chez nous ... Pour de bon! c'était ça, le malentendu: les Français pensaient que cette immigration était transitoire et que les jeunes étaient aussi des « immigrés ». Tout le monde se trompait ... D'ailleurs, nos parents voulaient qu'on reste dans notre identité maghrébine ...

Oui, quand je pense à toute cette histoire, avec du recul, je trouve que nous n'avons pas eu de chance, ni nous, ni la France ... Un ami de Goussainville, 45 ans, nous appelle « les blessés de la France » ... Je trouve qu'il a raison. C'est vrai, nous sommes blessés. Et nous n'avons même pas le droit de nous plaindre des injustices, parce qu'il y cette chose, là, qu'on a inventée pour nous couper la parole, la « victimisation » ... Et voilà comment je comprends quand je lis, après les attentats de janvier 2015 à Paris, que des jeunes dans les cités disent « *Nous ne sommes pas Charlie* », je comprends ce qu'ils veulent dire ... Ils veulent dénoncer l'apartheid dans lequel la France les a installés depuis trente ans ... l'islamophobie ... banalisée chez les politiques ... Oui, nous sommes blessés, les anciens comme beaucoup de jeunes ... Nous sommes nés dans la guerre d'Algérie, et hélas, nous avons eu vingt ans au moment de la fin des trente glorieuses ... ce qui nous a rendus « visibles », ce qui a fait de nous des cibles, des boucs-émissaires ... Des Français qui souffraient de la crise économique nous disaient: « Retournez dans votre pays, Bicots! Ici il n'y a plus de travail pour vous! … » Ça faisait mal. Je l'ai écrit dans mes romans … En 73, 74, commencèrent les premières bagarres de jeunes contre la police dans les banlieues de Lyon … La crise économique, la guerre d'Algérie, l'indépendance de l'Algérie … faisaient de nous des parias dans le pays de notre naissance, *la douce France.*

Voilà la malchance … Nous sommes devenus visibles au moment où l'économie était en déclin … la pire période. Avec la police, c'était déjà très difficile … Très difficile. Nous avons grandi dans la peur … dans les peurs … On comprend ainsi la haine des jeunes des cités contre ceux qui, au nom de la République, n'ont cessé d'énoncer des propos hypocrites et des promesses non tenues …

Je terminerai avec cette importante question: combien y-a-t-il de musulmans en France aujourd'hui? Moi, je dis, comme les Maoris et les *African-Americans*: entre 15–20% de la population totale. Mon père, par exemple, était algérien. Dans les statistiques officielles, il était identifié comme Algérien … Mais moi et mes six frères et sœurs, nous sommes français, et nous ne sommes plus visibles dans les statistiques. Mais nous sommes musulmans dans la mesure où nous avons le sentiment d'être ciblés et stigmatisés en tant que tels, quelles que soient nos croyances (ou non-croyances) religieuses. Nous avons fait des enfants, qui ont eux-mêmes fait des enfants et aujourd'hui nous sommes plus d'une cinquantaine de personnes, tous musulmans dans le sens que j'ai indiqué, mais français de nationalité…. Qu'est-ce que cela veut dire? Que des millions de personnes peuvent, lorsque l'islamophobie atteint un niveau insupportable comme c'est le cas aujourd'hui, dire: « Maintenant ça suffit! Stop. Nous sommes musulmans, nous aussi! … « *I'm Black and I'm proud! Say it Loud…!* » Toujours le modèle américain qui revient …

Voilà. Je veux dire que l'islamophobie en France est en train … depuis la première page du *Figaro magazine* en 1985 … ça ne date pas d'aujourd'hui … de créer un communautarisme musulman, même auprès de ceux qui ne sont pas musulmans, ou qui ne se revendiquent pas de l'Islam … même des laïcs…! Des millions de français d'origine maghrébine, beaucoup plus que les fameux 5 millions dont on nous parle depuis les années 60 … Combien de Harkis, en France et leurs enfants et les enfants de leurs enfants? Combien de Turcs, et leurs enfants et enfants de leurs enfants? Combien de Maliens, Sénégalais et autres Subsahariens? Combien de Comoriens? Combien? Des millions…, mais ils sont invisibles … ils votent peu … l'enjeu du vote obligatoire est là …

Si, face à cette absence remarquable, on ose évoquer … la « discrimination positive », on provoque immédiatement des réactions violentes … les conservateurs sortent l'artillerie républicaine conceptuelle … « Oh non! » La République n'a pas besoin de statistiques ethniques … les incantations sont toujours à l'œuvre, aussi fortes qu'inefficaces …

Résultat de tout ce gâchis ... beaucoup de jeunes des cités, d'origine maghrébine, s'exilent, comme leurs grands-parents l'ont fait en venant en France ... Ils vont travailler dans les pays anglophones, au Qatar, Dubai, en Chine, en Thaïlande...où ils ne sont pas « un problème », mais une « solution » ... où leur apparence physique n'est pas un préjudice ...

Hier, quand je suis arrivé à Luton airport, j'ai vu au guichet des contrôles de passeport un agent noir et un Sikh, côte à côte, qui vérifiaient les passeports des passagers ... avec – [Azouz Begag mime un turban] – J'ai aimé ça, cette belle image ... Et beaucoup de jeunes Français d'origine « visible » ... aiment ça, être invisibles, et s'exilent dans des pays où seuls leurs talents et leurs mérites vont véritablement faire la différence pour trouver un travail ... ce qu'ils n'ont pas trouvé en France ...

La France n'a pas été au rendez-vous ... J'ai compris que l'immigration était un miroir dans lequel se reflètent toutes les contradictions de la société de l'égalité, la liberté et la fraternité ... C'est un miroir ... Et la France, aujourd'hui, est en mauvais état ... Quant à moi, je vais continuer à écrire des livres, en français, je vais continuer à aller dans les quartiers pauvres pour dire aux gens: « Il faut lire, c'est le secret. Allez dans les bibliothèques, envolez-vous, lisez ... votez! » C'est mon travail, je continue, malgré Nicolas Sarkozy, malgré Brice Hortefeux, Nadine Morano, Christian Estrosi ... Brice Hortefeux, qui tous les mercredis matins durant le conseil des Ministres à l'Élysée – [Azouz Begag mime un signe d'égorgement] – me faisait ça, à moi, ministre de la promotion de l'égalité des chances! Ce sont des voyous! ... Ils me prenaient pour un mouton dans leur baignoire ... et voulaient m'égorger ... ces gens-là ont fait croire aux Français que leur problème était « le jeune des banlieues »! Donc, pour éviter d'être considérés comme des moutons ... je conseille aux musulmans de devenir végétariens s'ils veulent être intégrés en politique ... [Rires et applaudissements du public.]

Propos d'Azouz Begag retranscrits par
Melanie Bhend (University of Nottingham)

Nottingham French Studies 54.3 (2015): 340–341
DOI: 10.3366/nfs.2015.0131
© University of Nottingham
www.euppublishing.com/journal/nfs

NOTES ON CONTRIBUTORS

AZOUZ BEGAG, sociologue et écrivain, a servi de 2005 à 2007 comme Ministre délégué à l'égalité des chances. Chercheur au CNRS, il est l'auteur de nombreux ouvrages et articles sur les populations d'origine immigrée en milieu urbain. Depuis la parution du *Gone du Chaâba* en 1986 il a publié une vingtaine de romans et d'albums de bande dessinée. Il est aujourd'hui Conseiller Culturel de l'Ambassade de France au Portugal et Directeur de l'Institut Français de Lisbonne.
Address for correspondence: azouz.begag@orange.fr

PHILIP DINE is Personal Professor and Head of French at the National University of Ireland, Galway. He has published widely on representations of the French colonial empire, including particularly decolonization, in fields ranging from children's literature to professional sport. His other published research reflects more broadly on leisure and popular culture in France. He was the principal researcher for a collaborative project funded by the Irish Research Council on 'Sport and Identity in France' (2006–9).
Address for correspondence: School of Languages, Literatures and Cultures (French), National University of Ireland, Galway, University Road, Galway, Ireland; philip.dine@nuigalway.ie

CHARLES FORSDICK is James Barrow Professor of French at the University of Liverpool, and has been Arts and Humanities Research Council Theme Leadership Fellow for 'Translating Cultures' since 2012. He has published on exoticism, travel writing, postcolonial literature, histories of slavery, and the Francophone Caribbean (especially Haiti). He was, from 2012–14, President of the Society for French Studies.
Address for correspondence: Department of Modern Languages and Cultures, Cypress Building, University of Liverpool, Liverpool, L69 7ZR; craf@liv.ac.uk

YVAN GASTAUT est maître de conférences à l'université de Nice, membre du laboratoire URMIS (Unité de Recherches Migrations et Société), membre du Conseil d'Orientation du Musée de l'immigration. Il est notamment l'auteur de *L'Immigration et l'opinion en France sous la Ve République* (Paris: Seuil, 2000), et de *Le Métissage par le foot: l'intégration, mais jusqu'où?* (Paris: Autrement, 2008).
Address for correspondence: Yvan Gastaut, Université de Nice Sophia Antipolis, Campus Saint Jean d'Angely SJA3 / MSHS, 24 avenue des Diables bleus, 06357 Nice CEDEX 4, France; gastaut@unice.fr

ALEC G. HARGREAVES is Emeritus Professor of Transcultural French Studies at Florida State University. A specialist on post-colonial minorities in France, he has authored and edited numerous works including *Immigration and Identity in Beur Fiction: Voices from the North African Immigrant Community in France*, 2nd edn (Oxford: Berg, 1997), *Multi-Ethnic France: Immigration, Politics, Culture and Society* (London: Routledge, 2007), and *Transnational French Studies: Postcolonialism and 'Littérature-monde'*, co-edited with Charles Forsdick and David Murphy (Liverpool University Press, 2010).

Address for correspondence: Department of Modern Languages, Florida State University, Tallahassee, FL 32306, United States; ahargreaves@fsu.edu

DAVID MURPHY is Professor of French and Postcolonial Studies at the University of Stirling. He has written widely on Francophone African culture and has co-edited several collections on postcolonial theory, including *Francophone Postcolonial Studies: A Critical Introduction* (Arnold, 2003) and *Postcolonial Thought in the French-Speaking World* (Liverpool UP, 2009). In 2012, he published a critical edition of the collected writings of the Senegalese anti-colonial militant, Lamine Senghor (L'Harmattan). He is currently preparing a biography of Senghor for Verso.

Address for correspondence: Pathfoot E24, School of Arts and Humanities, University of Stirling, Stirling, FK9 4LA, Scotland; d.f.murphy@stir.ac.uk

CARRIE TARR is Emerita Professor of Film at Kingston University, UK. Her publications on ethnicity, identity, gender and sexuality in postcolonial French and Francophone cinema(s) include: *Cinema and the Second Sex: Women's Filmmaking in France in the 1980s and 1990s* (with B. Rollet, 2001); *Reframing Difference: 'beur' and 'banlieue' cinema in France* (2005); a special issue of *Modern & Contemporary France* on 'French Cinema: Transnational Cinema?' (2007); and a special issue of *Studies in French Cinema* on 'Women's Filmmaking in France 2000–2010' (2012).

Address for correspondence: c.tarr@kingston.ac.uk

CATHERINE WIHTOL DE WENDEN est Directrice de recherche au CNRS (CERI Sciences-po). Elle enseigne à Sciences-po et à l'Université La Sapienza de Rome. Politologue et juriste, elle a présidé le Research Committee 31 de l'Association européenne de Sociologie. Elle est l'auteur de nombreux articles et ouvrages scientifiques sur la politique d'immigration en France, la politique européenne des migrations, les frontières, la citoyenneté, la mondialisation des migrations et la gouvernance mondiale des migrations.

Address for correspondence: CERI, 56 rue Jacob, 75006 Paris, France; catherine.wihtoldewenden@sciencespo.fr

Index:
Nottingham French Studies 54 (2015)